Who Told You That You Were Naked?

Study Guide

Kelvin J. Cochran

3G Publishing, Inc.
Loganville, GA 30052
www.3gpublishinginc.com
Phone: 1-888-442-9637

First published by 3G Publishing, Inc. June, 2019

ISBN: 978-1-941247-54-9

Printed in the United States of America

Contents

About the Author

Kelvin J. Cochran is a native of Shreveport, LA, who now calls Atlanta, GA his home. He is a devout Christian man pursuing the life of a Psalm 112 man and the promises of Deuteronomy 28:1-14. His greatest desire is to fulfill the purpose of God for his life and to be living proof of God's exceeding great and precious promises.

Kelvin is a husband and father of three, with one granddaughter; and a faithful member of Elizabeth Baptist Church, Atlanta, GA where he serves as a deacon and teacher. He has thirty-four years in the Fire Service and has served as Fire Chief for the City of Shreveport Fire Department (LA); United States Fire Administrator (Washington, D.C.) and is former Fire Chief of the City of Atlanta Fire Rescue Department (GA).

Acknowledgment

I thank God for choosing me to deliver this message to redeemed men of the Body of Christ who wrestle with the stronghold of condemnation. I pray also that by the grace of God it will find its way into the hands of men who have not confessed Christ as Savior and Lord. While I am still a work in progress, my life is a testimony of the struggle with condemnation and how a man can grow from strength to strength, through diligent pursuit of fulfilling God's purpose for his life through the Word of God.

My wife Carolyn and my children Tiffane, Kelton and Camille, and my granddaughter Thailynn, inspire me day by day, to be the man God has called me to be. Their love and support keeps me striving for greater heights and depths of seeking the glory of God for our household and the generations of Cochrans to come.

The men in my bible study small group on Friday mornings at Q-Time Restaurant and the men of my Quest for Authentic Manhood small group at Elizabeth Baptist Church both inspired me to take what was initially a six week lesson plan to study this topic, to a book. Sharing the lesson plan with my brothers on Friday mornings convinced me that more men would be blessed from this study.

To God be the glory for what happens from here!

Introduction

During a six-month men's small group study of *"The Quest for Authentic Manhood"*, from the Men's Fraternity Series by Dr. Robert Lewis, Session 15: Genesis and Manhood, Part I focused on God's purpose for creating man. As the facilitator of the session, I was fascinated when the men begin to share their thoughts on the consequences of Adam's decision from then until now. It became quite clear that the generational consequences of the sinful nature are still in full effect—even for men who have been redeemed.

From your personal experience, identify three examples of the generational consequences of the sinful nature that is still in full effect—even for men who have been redeemed. (p.ix)

1. ______________________________________
2. ______________________________________
3. ______________________________________

God ___________ them with coats of skin through the shedding of ___________ of an innocent lamb. This redemptive solution would have ________________ implications for all of mankind.

What are the generational consequences of God's response to what Adam did in the Garden of Eden? (p.x)

1. ______________________________________
2. ______________________________________
3. ______________________________________

Adam hid behind a tree because he did not want to face the consequences of what he had done. What are examples of modern-day

And the eyes of both of them were opened, and they knew that they were naked and they sewed fig leaves together and made themselves loin coverings. They heard the sound of the Lord God walking in the garden in the cool of the day, and the man and his wife hid from the presence of the Lord God among the trees of the garden. Then the Lord God called the man and said to him. "Where are you?" He said, "I heard the sound of you in the garden, and I was afraid because I was naked; so I hid." And he said, ***"Who told you that you were naked?" Genesis 3:7-11***

Notes:

hiding places for men who do not want to face the consequences of their sinful nature?

1. ______________________________
2. ______________________________
3. ______________________________

"Who told you that you were naked?" is asking about more than the absence of clothing.

Circle the correct answer. (p. x)

True / False

List the four fundamental meanings of the word "naked": (pp. x-xi)

1. ______________________________
2. ______________________________
3. ______________________________
4. ______________________________

Overcoming the Stronghold of Condemnation

"In the world ye shall have tribulations: but be of good cheer; I have overcome the world." ***John 16:33***

As sons of God, we must share in the experience of Christ's <u>tribulations</u>. His <u>overcoming</u> gives us courage and confidence. In his <u>conquering</u> power we will walk in victory, unharmed and untouched by the evil one and his power. Fill in the blanks with one of the following words. (p. xii)

1. Overcoming
2. Conquering
3. Tribulations

Overcoming defined is:

1. To get the better of in a ____________ or ____________; conquer; defeat—to ____________ the enemy.

Notes:

2. To ____________ over (opposition, a debility, temptations, etc.); surmount—to overcome one's ____________ .
3. To ____________ or ____________ in body or mind, as does liquor, a drug, exertion, or emotion—overcome with guilt.
4. To ____________ or overrun.
5. To gain the ____________ : win; conquer—a plan to_____ by any means possible.

Stronghold defined is:

1. A ____________
2. A ____________

Through the act of one man's offense death has reigned by one man. (p. xii)

Circle one: Adam / Jesus

We who have received the abundance of grace and the gift of righteousness shall reign in life by one man. (p. xii)

Circle one: Adam / Jesus

Choose the word from the list below to complete the sentences:

Many sons of God are not reigning in life victoriously because we are overcome with the stronghold of ____________ . (pp. xii-xiii)

Men who suffer with the ____________ of condemnation have placed more emphasis on what ____________ did in the Garden of Eden than what ____________ did on Calvary. (p. xiii)

The greatest weapon the enemy has against a man after he has made a confession of faith is ____________________.

1. Jesus
2. Condemnation
3. Affliction
4. Adam
5. Confession of faith

Chapter 1

The Fall into Condemnation

When the woman saw that the tree was good for food, and that it was a delight to the eyes, and that it was desirable to make one wise, she took from its fruit and ate; and she gave also to her husband with her, and he ate. Then the eyes of both of them were open, and they knew that they were naked; (Genesis 3:6-7a)

The Origin of Condemnation

God established Adam as the chief ___________ , the earthblesser. He had ___________ over everything God created. God ___________ Adam to prosper in all things. (p. 15)

God created the Garden of Eden and placed Adam and Eve there, to cultivate it and to keep it. They were both physically naked (Genesis 2:25) but spiritually clothed. Their spiritual clothing consisted of: (p. 15). Fill in the blanks.

1. ________________
2. ________________
3. ________________
4. ________________

The act of disobedience in the Garden changed how Adam saw himself and how God saw him. In God's eyes, the clothing of glory, holiness, honor, and righteousness were gone. (p. 16)

Choose the word from the list below to complete the sentences:

1. Condemnation
2. Perfection
3. Deprivation

Adam's reaction to his spiritual demotion and his nakedness introduced guilt, fear, and death to what was formally ____________ . (p. 16)

_____________ and _____________ are the greatest barriers to a man walking in the fullness of his purpose and in the fullness of his calling.

When the woman saw that the tree was good for food, and that it was a delight to the eyes, and that the tree was desirable to make one wise, she took from its fruit and ate; and she gave also to her husband with her, and he ate. The eyes of both of them were opened, and they knew that they were naked; Genesis 3:6-7a

Adam and his wife were both naked, and they felt no shame. Genesis 2:25

The mindset that Adam had after his sin was that nakedness is: (p. 16). Fill in the blanks.

1. ________________
2. ________________
3. ________________

Adam's realization of what he had done caused which of the following to occur:

1. A deep disappointment he had never experienced
2. Doubt of the excellence and perfection of God
3. A loss that was greater than what was gained
4. An overwhelming conviction that things would never be the same
5. All of the above

List four important facts about condemnation (p. 17)

1. ____
2. ____
3. ____
4. ____

We know that the whole creation has been groaning as in the pains of childbirth right up to the present time. Romans 8:22

Eerdman's Dictionary of the Bible indicates that some New Testament writings characterize man's choice of sin as a *"fall under condemnation of the devil"* or a *"fall under condemnation"*.

Not a novice, lest being lifted up with pride he ***fall into condemnation of the devil.*** *(I Timothy 3:6);*

Pride was one of three temptations which caused Eve to eat the forbidden fruit. She was told by the serpent she would be like God, knowing good and evil. This scripture indicates that condemnation originated from the devil and is sustained by the devil.

But above all things, my brethren, swear not, neither by heaven, neither by the earth, neither by any other oath: but let your yea be yea; and your nay, nay; ***lest ye fall into condemnation****. (James 5:12).*

When a man does not keep his word or makes a vow or an oath with wrong motives, there is potential for that man to fall into condemnation.

Condemnation occurred when Adam ate, not Eve. Their eyes were opened and they saw that they were naked.

Since both Adam and Eve were forbidden to eat the fruit from the Tree of the Knowledge of Good and Evil, why is it that their eyes were opened only after Adam had taken a bite?

____

____

____

____

Are there situations today where husbands are responsible for the actions of their wives? If yes, provide an example.

____

____

____

____

Sin changed their predominantly spiritual condition to a predominately physical condition. They were both overwhelmed with a sense of doom and loss. (p. 18)

Adam and Eve lost benefits of being predominantly spiritual after they ate of the forbidden fruit. List five losses associated with spiritual demotion. (p. 18)

Losses Associated with Spiritual Demotion: (p. 18)

1. ______________________________________
2. ______________________________________
3. ______________________________________
4. ______________________________________
5. ______________________________________

Read: Acts 11:12-14 (The Household of Cornelius)

12 The Spirit told me to have no hesitation about going with them. These six brothers also went with me, and we entered the man's house. 13 He told us how he had seen an angel appear in his house and say, 'Send to Joppa for Simon who is called Peter. 14 He will bring you a message through which you and all your household will be saved.'

Read: Acts 16:31-34 (The Household of the Jailer)

31 They replied, "Believe in the Lord Jesus, and you will be saved—you and your household." 32 Then they spoke the word of the Lord to him and to all the others in his house. 33 At that hour of the night the jailer took them and washed their wounds; then immediately he and all his household were baptized. 34 The jailer brought them into his house and set a meal before them; he was filled with joy because he had come to believe in God—he and his whole household.

For all of you who were baptized into Christ have clothed yourselves with Christ. ***Galatians 3:27***

19 Now the Lord God had formed out of the ground all the wild animals and all the birds in the sky. He brought them to the man to see what he would name them; and whatever the man called each living creature, that was its name. ***Genesis 2:19***

23 The man said, "This is now bone of my bones and flesh of my flesh; she shall be called 'woman,' for she was taken out of man." 24 That is why a man leaves his father and mother and is united to his wife, and they become one flesh. 25 Adam and his wife were both naked, and they felt no shame. ***Genesis 2:23-25***

As such, when a man is under condemnation, it affects his __________ and ___________ . However, when a man overcomes the stronghold of condemnation, his salvation blesses his wife and influences the atmosphere in his entire ___________ household. (p. 18)

Adam Before The Fall

Which of the following best describes Adam's status as a man before the fall? (p. 18)

1. Adam had a special habitat created by God to live and thrive in
2. Adam had a divine assignment given to him by God
3. Adam had authority over everything God created
4. Adam was given Eve before God gave him a job

Circle the correct answer:

a. 1, 2 and 4 b. 1, 2 and 3 c. 1, 3 and 4

Choose the word from the list below to complete the sentences:

a. Jesus b. Adam

Sin entered creation through _____________ . Salvation entered creation through _____________ . We are all natural born sinners.

Circle the correct answer:

Through Christ, we are born again into righteousness. Men who are still in the nature of Adam are (naked/clothed). Men who are in the nature of Christ are (naked/clothed). (p. 19)

The naked mindset places greater emphasis on what Adam did. The clothed mindset places greater emphasis on what Jesus has done.

Place a check under the name which corresponds to the description that most accurately distinguish Jesus from Adam. (p. 19)

Description	Adam	Jesus
Son of God		
Made flesh from dirt		
Made flesh from Spirit		
Nature of Sin		
Nature of Righteousness		
Condemnation		
Redemption		
Deprivation		
Restoration		
Naked		
Clothed		

Nakedness Defined

Eerdman's Dictionary definition of naked is:

____

____

____

____

Read Leviticus 18:1-23; 20:10-21; Ezekiel 16:8. In your own words, describe the biblical definition of nakedness.

____

____

____

____

Nakedness is used to describe a variety of human conditions associated with our sinful nature, however, the two words which categorize most of these conditions are condemnation and deprivation (p. 20)

If a man commits adultery with another man's wife—with the wife of his neighbor—both the adulterer and the adulteress are to be put to death... ***Lev. 20:10-21***

Later I passed by, and when I looked at you and saw that you were old enough for love, I spread the corner of my garment over you and covered your naked body... ***Ezek. 16:8***

The beast and the ten horns you saw will hate the prostitute. They will bring her to ruin and leave her naked; they will eat her flesh and burn her with fire. ***Rev. 17:16***

Saul's anger flared up at Jonathan and he said to him, "You son of a perverse and rebellious woman! Don't I know that you have sided with the son of Jesse to your own shame and to the shame of the mother who bore you? ***1 Sam. 20:30***

Nakedness symbolized adulterers (1 Samuel 20:30) and prostitutes (Ezekiel 16:36- 37; Revelation 17:16). In this sense, which of the following categories of people are naked?

1. Adulterers
2. Prostitutes
3. People who reject God
4. All of the above

Nakedness in the sense of being inadequately clothed is one of several types of deprivations used to represent which of the following? (Underline all that apply.)

1. Poverty
2. Oppression
3. Judgment
4. Punishment
5. None of the above

Being fully clothed was a requirement for priests during the performance of their temple duties. They had to be completely covered. If any part of their body was exposed during their holy duties in the temple before our holy God the penalty was death.

Choose the word from the list below to complete the sentences:

1. covered
2. condemnation
3. deprivation
4. clothed

Being spiritually ____________ or ____________ is an absolute imperative for meaningful interaction with God. (p.21)

The Fall has created two human conditions which initiated and continues to widen the gap between God and man. The two conditions are ________________ and ______________ . Combined, they constitute the naked condition. (p. 21)

Notes:

The Naked Condition

The naked condition of condemnation describes the adverse _______ and _________ consequences associated with nakedness. Which of the following are associated with the human condition of condemnation? (p. 21)

1. A death sentence
2. A sense of being unworthy
3. A sense of being inadequate
4. A sense of hopelessness
5. All the above

____________ is the twin brother of condemnation. It describes the adverse spiritual, psychological, and ________ ________ associated with nakedness. Deprivation is removal from ecclesiastical office with all its ________ and ________ . Which of the following are associated with the human condition of deprivation? (p.22)

1. Dispossession
2. Hardship
3. Not enough
4. A never-ending quest to be fulfilled
5. All the above

All men are infected with the sinful nature. Condemnation and deprivation are the drivers that result in many afflictions and many infirmities for men; not one of us is immune.

As men, we overcome by the blood of the Lamb and by the word of our testimony. In the spirit of transparency and confession, list the conditions of deprivation you are struggling with as a man. (pp. 22-23)

They sailed to the region of the Gerasenes,[a] which is across the lake from Galilee. 27 When Jesus stepped ashore, he was met by a demon-possessed man from the town. For a long time this man had not worn clothes or lived in a house, but had lived in the tombs. 28 When he saw Jesus, he cried out and fell at his feet, shouting at the top of his voice, "What do you want with me, Jesus, Son of the Most High God? I beg you, don't torture me!" 29 For Jesus had commanded the impure spirit to come out of the man. 35 and the people went out to see what had happened. When they came to Jesus, they found the man from whom the demons had gone out, sitting at Jesus' feet, dressed and in his right mind; and they were afraid.
*...**Luke 8:26-29, 35***

Conditions of Deprivation I Personally Struggle with as a Man:

1. ____________________
2. ____________________
3. ____________________
4. ____________________
5. ____________________

Biblical Men with Deprived Experiences

Don't be discouraged about your struggles. Discouragement itself is a symptom of condemnation. You are not alone. Many of our biblical heroes also had challenges in these areas. Beside each condition, list one man from the Bible who struggled in that area: (p. 23)

1. Fatherhood ____________________
2. Addictions ____________________
3. Jealousy ____________________
4. Temptation ____________________
5. Reconciliation ____________________
6. Depression ____________________
7. Stubbornness ____________________

The Clothed Condition

Salvation through Jesus Christ reverses all the effects of The Fall and provides a spiritual transformation from the naked condition to the clothed condition. (p. 25)

Choose the word from the list below to complete the sentences:

1. Righteous nature
2. Human condition
3. Sin nature
4. Spiritual condition

Being born again changes our ____________________ and restores a man to his dominate ____________________. We die to the nature of Adam—the ____________________. We inherit the nature of Christ—the ____________________. (p. 25)

Notes:

Through the first Adam, we are natural born sinners. When we are born again through faith in Jesus Christ—the second Adam, we are spiritually reborn to a nature of righteousness. Just as the physiological DNA of Adam's carnality dominated our flesh, those of us who have been born again have the Spiritual DNA of God taking residence in our body dominating our flesh.

Through this divine regeneration, we become sons of God.

To make this plain, match the word to the correct phrase. (p. 25)

1. The ______ of God	a. sons
2. Became the ______ of man	b. sons
3. In order that the ______ of men	c. Son
4. May become the ______ of God	d. Son

The blood of Jesus severed the blood lineage of our humanity. We are no longer identified by the nature of Adam in God's eyes. We are identified by the nature of _____________.

Because the bloodline of our humanity has been severed by the blood of Jesus, everything about us has been spiritually transformed. We are no longer the men we used to be. Our relationship with the Father is not through genealogical lineage.

In the case of Abraham, Isaac, and Jacob—Jacob is Abraham's grandson through genealogical lineage. Because of Christ, our relationship with the Father is not linked through a chain of genealogy. Jesus is God's son. I am God's son and my son is God's son. We are in the direct lineage of God the Father as sons _____________ by the Spirit of God. We are _____________with Christ. (p. 25)

Notes:

To summarize Chapter 1, match the phrases below:

1. Naked Condition	a. God-consciousness
2. Clothed Condition	b. Condemnation
3. Naked Condition	c. Redeemed
4. Clothed Condition	d. World-consciousness
5. Naked Condition	e. Restored
6. Clothed Condition	f. Deprivation

Case Study: Jesus and a Naked Man

In the case study of Jesus and the naked man. List some things about his life that might be evidenced in the lives of men today.

1. ____
2. ____
3. ____
4. ____

What did God say to you personally in Chapter 1?

____
____
____
____

Write a short prayer to God based on what you have heard from Him.

Heavenly Father:

____
____
____
____

In Jesus Name—Amen!!!

Chapter 2

The Naked

But Jesus said unto him, "Follow me; and let the dead (spiritually dead) bury their dead (physically dead). Matthew 8:22

Notes:

The naked is a phrase which applies to all who are ____________. The place of origin of spiritual death for all humankind is the _______. From the time of The Fall until now, all are born spiritually dead. The one who instigated spiritual death is _________. The progenitor (ancestor) of spiritual death is Adam.

The serpent's provocative conversation led to Eve's transgression, but nothing happened until Adam took the forbidden fruit and ate it. They became spiritually dead.

Circle the phrase which describes the change that occurred in Adam and Eve as a result of sin. (p.29)

1. They lost	a. spiritual awareness / carnal-awareness
2. They became more	b. God-conscious / self-conscious

Choose the word from the list below to complete the sentences:

1. Promises
2. Disobedient
3. Pleasures
4. Deceitfulness

The ____________ of sin is the sense we will gain more from the ____________ act than what we already have—that the ____________ of sin are greater than the ____________ of God.

Is there ever a time when giving in to temptation results in a blessing? Explain.

____

____

____

____

As men of God, we have been struggling to see ourselves as God sees us since The Fall. Many men are wandering aimlessly and do not know why, but it is due to the mentality of nakedness. The naked mentality is of the devil. He is the father of lies and he is still up to his old deceptive tricks, trying to convince us that we are naked even though we are clothed in the righteousness of Christ.

The answer to the question, "Who told you that you were naked?" which God posed to Adam is—no one! Because of spiritual death by sin, Adam simply lost his mind, the mind he had before he sinned. He lost the ability to see himself as God saw him.

Condemnation still causes too many Christian men today to see ourselves as God sees us. For many of us, it's hard to grasp the fact that Jesus Christ paid the full price for our sins and that we are always in right standing with God.

List three factors that make it difficult for a man to see himself as God sees him. (p. 30)

1. ______________________________
2. ______________________________
3. ______________________________

The Naked Mentality

The naked mentality was evident in the religious leaders, the scribes, and the Pharisees during Jesus' ministry on earth. They believed their righteousness was based upon keeping the law and rooted in their ancestral bloodline through Abraham. Jesus could not convince them otherwise.

Likewise, many Christians today are convinced that salvation is of Jesus Christ, but that it is still necessary to keep the law in order to be righteous. The Word of God cannot convince them otherwise.

To believe in Jesus Christ and yet believe we are condemned—that we are still sinners who must work or keep the law to be righteous before God is a condition of nakedness.

10 He answered, "I heard you in the garden, and I was afraid because I was naked; so I hid."
11 And he said, "Who told you that you were naked? Have you eaten from the tree that I commanded you not to eat from?"
12 The man said, "The woman you put here with me—she gave me some fruit from the tree, and I ate it."
Gen. 3:10-12

"But Jesus said unto him, Follow me; and let the dead (spiritually dead) bury their own dead (physically dead)."
Matthews 8:22

"Come to me, all you who are weary and burdened, and I will give you rest."
Matthew 11:28

As for you, you were dead in your transgressions and sins, 2 in which you used to live when you followed the ways of this world and of the ruler of the kingdom of the air, the spirit who is now at work in those who are disobedient. 3 All of us also lived among them at one time, gratifying the cravings of our flesh[a] and following its desires and thoughts. Like the rest, we were by nature deserving of wrath. 4 But because of his great love for us, God, who is rich in mercy.
Eph. 2:1-4

Choose the word from the list below to complete the sentences:

1. Self-condemnation
2. Self-deprivation

The naked mentality of this sort becomes a conscious choice made by a believer and is commonly referred to as ____________ and ____________. It is a decision to not accept what Christ has done, even after coming into the knowledge of the truth. (p. 32)

Which of the following describes a clothed man with a naked mentality regarding salvation in Jesus Christ?

a. He came, but he did not accomplish.
b. He came, but he did not finish.
c. He came, but he failed.
d. All the above

Choose the word from the list below to complete the sentences:

1. Naked mentality
2. Transgressions
3. Condemned
4. Saved
5. Everlasting
6. Forevermore
7. Utmost

The ________________ exists when sons of God feel the strength of our salvation only between ________________ . In other words, we only feel ________________ until the next time we mess up, then we feel ________________ all over again. (p. 33)

Salvation is continuous, ongoing, and ________________ .

We are not forgiven for the time being. We are forgiven __________. We are not saved to the almost. We are saved to the __________. (p. 33)

Select the answer most appropriate to these statements. (p. 34)

1. There is no such thing as more or less righteous.
   a. True
   b. False

2. There is no such thing as being more or less a sinner.
   a. True
   b. False

3. We are either "righteous" or "sinner".
   a. True
   b. False

4. The act of disobedience by Adam in the Garden of Eden made all men sinners.
   a. True
   b. False

5. The act of obedience by Jesus on Calvary made all men who believe on him righteous.
   a. True
   b. False

All the statements above are true. We are not half saved. We are not partially redeemed. Our salvation and redemption are complete. We are fully clothed, not half naked.

Men who resist seeking the presence and will of God for their lives are acting on the instinct of the sin nature received from Adam. Just as Adam hid in the Garden behind a tree with fig leaves for a covering, men today are hiding themselves and have many forms of coverings—modern-day fig leaves.

To the angel[a] of the church in Sardis write:

These are the words of him who holds the seven spirits[b] of God and the seven stars. I know your deeds; you have a reputation of being alive, but you are dead. ***Rev. 3:1***

Notes:

List examples of modern-day fig leaves men use for covering and hiding. (p. 35)

1. ____________________
2. ____________________
3. ____________________
4. ____________________

List any fig leaves you might have in your life.

1. ____________________
2. ____________________
3. ____________________
4. ____________________

Let's pray. Heavenly Father: Thank you for exposing the fig leaves in my life. Forgive me for trying to use worldly coverings to cover my nakedness and to satisfy my need for being accepted and whole. I am thankful that I am clothed with Christ. In him I have all I need for life and godliness. Amen.

For a man to continue to carry the weight of the sin nature and the burden of condemnation after receiving Christ is an indication of his continuous struggle with nakedness mentality. (p. 36)

For all of you who were baptized into Christ have clothed yourselves with Christ. ***Gal. 3:27***

Place an "S" for salvation or a "C" for condemnation at the end of the sentence which best describes it. (p. 37)

1. Expects something bad to happen ______.
2. Expects something good to happen ______.
3. Is rooted in fear and doubt ______.
4. Is rooted in faith and confidence ______.
5. Is hell on earth ______.
6. Is heaven on earth ______.

Name five indicators of the naked mentality. (p. 37)

1. ______________________________
2. ______________________________
3. ______________________________
4. ______________________________

Match the definition to the appropriate state of consciousness. (p. 37)

1. The consciousness a man experiences through his physical body
   a. World-consciousness
   b. Self-consciousness
   c. God-consciousness

2. The consciousness a man experiences through his soul
   a. World-consciousness
   b. Self-consciousness
   c. God-consciousness

3. The consciousness a man experiences through his spirit
   a. World-consciousness
   b. Self-consciousness
   c. God-consciousness

CASE STUDY: The Emperor's New Clothes

Of the three states of consciousness, which one(s) best describes the mindset of the Emperor. Explain.

____
____
____
____

Notes:

Notes:

Why would the Emperor continue the public procession even after the truth of his nakedness was revealed?

Of the three states of consciousness, which one most accurately describe your mindset. Explain.

What did God say to you in Chapter 2?

Write what you want to say to God based on what you have heard him say to you.

Heavenly Father:

Chapter 3

The Need for Covering

And the eyes of them both were opened, and they knew that they were naked; and they sowed fig leaves together and made themselves aprons. Genesis 3:7

The Lord God made garments of skin for Adam and his wife and clothed them.
Gen. 3:21

Adam's covering (Genesis 3:7) was aprons made of fig leaves. The Hebrew word for covering is "chagorah" which means, something with which to be gird about, as a belt or girdle. This man-made apron of leaves was inadequate to cover their nakedness. This fig leaves were temporary and incomplete. They would eventually become withered, shrink, dry out and die. The fig leaves did not adequately cover their nakedness, nor did it provide the protection they needed. More importantly, Adam's solution of fig leaves did not restore this relationship with God.

Genesis 3:21 Unto Adam also and to his wife did the Lord God make coats of skins, and clothed them.

According to Genesis 3:21, God's solution to Adam and Eve's nakedness was to make them coats of skin.

What did God have to do in order to clothe Adam and Eve? (p. 43)

____

____

____

____

What is the significance of choosing a lamb and what made it a adequate solution to Adam and Eve's nakedness? (p. 44)

____

____

____

____

For all of you who were baptized into Christ have clothed yourselves with Christ.
Gal. 3:27

The lamb chosen by God was the foretaste of what was to come. The Lamb of God—Jesus Christ was sacrificed on Calvary, shed his blood, died and rose again. Galatians 3:27 says, those what have been baptized in Christ has been clothed with Christ.

Choose the word from the list below to complete the sentences:

1. Clothed
2. Mind
3. Putting on

____________ Christ is a renewing of the ____________, a constant awareness of our ____________ condition. Circle the human condition that is not aligned within the proper column. (p. 44)

Discovering the Human Condition of Nakedness

Adam's human reaction to the question, "Who told you that you were naked?" after hearing the voice of God resulted in three discoveries in the human condition of nakedness. Match the reaction to the appropriate human condition. (p. 45)

1. I was afraid ____ a. guilt discovered
2. I was naked ____ b. fear discovered
3. I hid myself ____ c. shame discovered

If the condition is in the wrong column, draw a line to indicate the correct column.

The Human Condition Before and After Sin	
Before Sin	**After Sin**
Afraid of God	Courageous in God
Confident	Ashamed
Guilty before God	Innocent in God
Clothed	Naked

The Origin of Doubt

A double-minded man is unstable in all his ways. James 1:8

Notes:

Now the serpent was more crafty than any of the wild animals the Lord God had made. He said to the woman, "Did God really say, 'You must not eat from any tree in the garden'?" **Gen. 3:1**

6 But when you ask, you must believe and not doubt, because the one who doubts is like a wave of the sea, blown and tossed by the wind. 7 That person should not expect to receive anything from the Lord. 8 Such a person is double-minded and unstable in all they do.
James 1:6-8

Choose the word from the list below to complete the sentences:

1. You Shall Not Surely Die
2. Truth
3. Word of God

One of the consequences of our depraved condition is we still have the propensity to doubt the truth of God, especially when the _______ of God conflict with the desires of our carnal nature. (p. 46)

The question raised by the serpent, "hath God said, ye shall not eat of every tree of the garden?" was asked with the specific intent of questioning the credibility and authenticity of the ___________ . The serpent's reply to Eve's affirmative response based on the truth was, " ___________________ "

Doubt initiated a series of events that eventually led to The Fall. Since the time of The Fall, mankind has struggled with accepting and standing on the truth of the Word of God over the Father of lies, the Devil. Match the biblical character with their experience in doubting the truth of God.

Choose the individual from the column that complete the sentences:

Judges 6:39

John 20:24-25

Exodus 3

- Doubted God could provide Abraham a baby through her in old age ___________
- Doubted God could use him to deliver Israel from bondage ___________
- Doubted God could use him to deliver Israel from the Amalekites ___________

Gideon

Thomas

Moses

- Doubted that God had chosen the right person to be king ____________ Sarah *Gen. 18:12*

- Doubted that Jesus Christ had risen fom the grave ____________ Saul ***1 Samuel 10:22***

Rate the statements below as "true" or "false" regarding doubt and a double-minded man.

1. Doubt is essentially questioning God's commitment to keep his word.
   a. True
   b. False
2. Doubt is questioning God's ability to keep his word.
   a. True
   b. False
3. Doubt is the absence of faith or the wavering between belief and unbelief.
   a. True
   b. False
4. Wavering between belief and unbelief is the condition of being double-minded.
   a. True
   b. False
5. A double-minded man is a man who is stable and fully confident in the Word of God.
   a. True
   b. False

The Origin of Fear

God has not given us the spirit of fear. 2 Timothy 1:7

Choose the word from the list below to complete the sentences:

1. Phobias
2. Fullness

Notes:

3. Condition
4. Distressing emotion

As a result of Adam's experience, men today have many ___________ persistent irrational fears of a specific object, activity, or situations which lead to a compelling desire to avoid them—most of which have little or no chance of actually happening.

Fear is a ___________ ___________ aroused by impending danger, evil, or pain whether the threat is real or imagined.

Fear is the feeling or ___________ of being afraid.

The fears born out of the sinful nature have caused many men to completely alter their lifestyle, resulting in behaviors which limit the capacity of God to manifest his ___________ in their lives. (p. 48)

Place in the proper blank which best describes it.

- o Fear of Self-disclosure
- o Fear of Commitment
- o Fear of Failure

______________________________ causes a man to go from one relationship to another, never get married, and go from one job to another.
______________________________ causes a man to not take risks which build his independence and wealth resulting in a mediocre life.
______________________________ causes a man to refrain from sharing personal challenges with family and friends.

List the fears that provide the greatest challenges in your life as a man?

1. ____
2. ____
3. ____

The Origin of Blame

The man said, "The woman you put here with me—she gave me the fruit from the tree, and I ate it. Genesis 3:12

The loss of Adam's spiritual nature created the infamous couple of fear and shame which conceived and gave birth to yet another consequence of our depraved condition—blame.

Rate the following statements as "true" or "false" regarding blame.

1. Blame is directly associated with a man's natural tendency to reject accountability.
   a. True
   b. False
2. Blame is a man's effort to cover up his own sin when he is caught, called out, or challenged for transgressions or violations of laws, rules or regulations.
   a. True
   b. False
3. Blame is an act of placing responsibility or fault on another person and an unwillingness to answer to another for what we have done.
   a. True
   b. False

Why is placing blame one of the first inclinations of a man who is caught, called out or challenged when experiencing a transgression or violating a rule or policy?

____

____

____

____

____

*The man said, "The woman you put here with me—she gave me some fruit from the tree, and I ate it." **Gen. 3:12***

Notes:

What did God say to you in Chapter 3?

Write what you want to say to God based upon what you have heard him say to you.

Heavenly Father:

Chapter 4

The Clothed

For all who were baptized into Christ have clothed yourselves with Christ. Galatians 3:27

Meanwhile we groan, longing to be clothed with our heavenly dwelling, because when we are clothed, we will not be found naked. 2 Corinthians 5:2-3

Notes:

The desire to be clothed has been a longing of men since The Fall. The overwhelming spiritual and emotional sense of loss of God's divine clothing was only partially and temporarily placated by Adam's solution of fig leaves. He was somewhat covered, but compared to his previous divine clothing, the fig leaves were woefully inadequate.

Adam's desire to clothe himself was motivated by a desire to restore himself to a state of being presentable before God and to cover up what he and Eve had done as if nothing ever happened.

Are men today still longing to restore themselves to a state of being presentable before God and to cover up transgressions as if nothing ever happened? If yes, explain.

____

____

____

____

____

What are modern day examples of man-made solutions for covering up transgressions and restoring right standing with God?

1. ____
2. ____
3. ____
4. ____

The Significance of Clothes

The primary purpose of clothing from the beginning until now is to _

____

____

____

____

____

Rate the following statements as "true" or "false" regarding the significance of clothing. (p. 55)

1. Clothes have a significant impact on how a man feels about himself.
   a. True
   b. False
2. Clothes play a significant role in the first impression a man makes on others.
   a. True
   b. False
3. Over time, a man's style of clothing does not play a part in the testimony of his personality and character.
   a. True
   b. False

Choose the word from the list below to complete the sentences:

1. Condemnation
2. Insecure
3. Unsure
4. Confidence
5. Ashamed
6. Embarrassed

When a man is inappropriately dressed he is ______________ , ______________, and lacks ______________. (p. 56)

If a man shows up at an event that has a specific dress code and is the only man in the wrong attire, he is ______________ and ______________.

These are the same emotional responses Adam experienced in the Garden of Eden and are consequences of ______________ or nakedness.

Jesus Clothes

A man without Christ is naked no matter how good he feels in his clothes.

Notes:

Notes:

God's perspective on clothes is different from man's view of clothing. To be in right standing with God we must have on the clothing he provides, the Lamb's clothing, Jesus clothes. (p.57)

Which of the following occasions are more suitable for Jesus clothes?

a. Good and bad occasions
b. Happy and sad occasions
c. Formal and casual occasions
d. All the above occasions

Being clothed with Christ makes us uniform in the mind of God. Which of the following best defines the word "uniform"?

a. Identical or consistent from example to example
b. Without variations in detail
c. An identifying outfit worn be members making everyone the same
d. All the above

Because we have been clothed with Christ we are uniform in the sight of God—all identical to the Son. We all look alike—we all look like Jesus Christ.

What are the similarities between the uniforms provided to firefighters and the uniforms for those who have been clothed with Christ?

____
____
____
____
____

List the five decrees of a clothed-minded man. (p.60)
1. I am____.
2. I am____.
3. I am____.
4. I am____.
5. I am____.

Notes:

What did God say to you in Chapter 4?

Write what you want to say to God based on what you have heard him say to you.

Heavenly Father:

Chapter 5

The Distinction Between the Clothed and the Naked

The Lord loves the righteous; but the way of the wicked he turns upside down. Psalm 146:8c-9c

Notes:

God makes a distinction between the clothed man and the naked man. These distinctions are made throughout scripture, but they are most prevalent in the Book of Psalms and the Book of Proverbs.

List the Biblical Synonyms for the clothed man and the naked man. (p. 61)

Distinctions Between The Clothed and The Naked	
The Clothed Man	**The Naked Man**

Choose the word from the list below to complete the sentences:

1. Double-minded
2. Naked
3. Cursed
4. Clothes
5. Anything
6. Blessed

The biblical distinctions make it clear—a man is either __________ through what Jesus did on Calvary or ______________ through what Adam did in the Garden of Eden. We cannot be ______________ with regard to our status of adornment before the Lord, thinking one minute we are clothed and the next minute we are naked. That man will not receive ______________ from the Lord. (p. 64)

The life of the clothed man is ______________. The life of the naked man is cursed. (p. 65)

From the Book of Deuteronomy 28, list five blessings of the clothed man.

1. ______________________________
2. ______________________________
3. ______________________________
4. ______________________________
5. ______________________________

From the Book of Deuteronomy 28, list five curses of the naked man.

1. ______________________________
2. ______________________________
3. ______________________________
4. ______________________________
5. ______________________________

The covenant makes a distinction between the clothed and the naked. Those who are diligently seeking the Lord and walking in his ways are the clothed. On the other hand, those who rebel against the Lord and walk in the ways of the world are naked.

Check the box which best describe the man you are.

- ☐ The Clothed Man
- ☐ The Naked Man
- ☐ Half Clothed/Half Naked

What did God say to you in Chapter 5?

____
____
____
____
____

Write what you want to say to God based on what you have heard him say to you.

Notes:

Notes:

Heavenly Father:

Chapter 6

Conviction and Condemnation

God is mighty, but does not despise men; he is mighty, and firm in his purpose. 6 He does not keep the wicked alive but gives the afflicted their rights. 7 He does not take his eyes off the righteous; he enthrones them with kings and exalts them forever. 8 But if men are bound in chains, held fast by cords of affliction, 9 He tells them what they have done—that they have sinned arrogantly. 10 He makes them listen to correction and commands them to repent of their evil. 11 If they obey and serve him, they will spend the rest of their days in prosperity and their years in contentment. 12 But if they do not listen, they will perish by the sword and die without knowledge. Job 36:5-12

5 God is mighty, but despises no one; he is mighty, and firm in his purpose.
6 He does not keep the wicked alive but gives the afflicted their rights. 7 He does not take his eyes off the righteous; he enthrones them with kings and exalts them forever.
8 But if people are bound in chains, held fast by cords of affliction, 9 he tells them what they have done—that they have sinned arrogantly. 10 He makes them listen to correction and commands them to repent of their evil.
11 If they obey and serve him, they will spend the rest of their days in prosperity and their years in contentment. 12 But if they do not listen, they will perish by the sword[a] and die without knowledge.
Job 36:5-12

Most men often confuse the spiritual response of conviction with the carnal response of condemnation.

Which word best fits the statement below? Fill in the blank with either conviction or condemnation. (p. 67)

________________________comes through God-consciousness.

________________________comes through sin-consciousness.

________________________is the awareness of God at the time of temptation to choose God's way.

________________________is a predominant awareness of the sinful nature and a compelling sense of being defeated by it.

________________________is the Holy Spirit reminding us of the commandments, precepts, statutes, and laws of God which illuminate the way out of temptation.

________________________is a reminder of what Adam did in the Garden of Eden.

________________________is a reminder of what Jesus did on Calvary.

God does not take his eyes off clothed men. He watches over them in order to perform his word in their lives. Which of the following is true (Circle the correct answer)? (p. 68)

a. If we become bound in chains and held back by cords or chains of affliction, through conviction, he tells us what we have done, but does not make us listen.
b. He brings promotions and advancements as he has promised according to our faithfulness to him.

If clothed men become bound in sinful patterns or addictions, how does God use conviction according to Job 36:5-12?

Notes:

Is it possible for a clothed man to continue down a path outside of God's purpose without hearing from God? Yes / No

When God provides instruction and corrective actions, what happens to the man who is faithful and obeys him?

For the clothed man, conviction is at work:

a. During the period of temptation
b. In the act of transgression
c. Immediately following a transgression
d. Conviction is at work before, during and after a transgression

Conviction is a: blessing/curse. Which statement best summarizes what we have learned about conviction?

a. Conviction is a heightened sense of awareness of our human weaknesses, tendencies, and shortcomings, coupled with the compelling sense that we are victorious.
b. Conviction is our Mentor and Guide through the Holy Spirit.
c. Both statements summarize the truth about conviction.

When a man fails to listen to the voice of conviction, it leads to which of the following: (p. 69)

a. Yielding to temptation
b. Transgressions
c. Condemnation
d. All the above

Notes:

Condemnation is a blessing/curse. Which of the following statements best summarize what we have learned about condemnation?

a. Condemnation attempts to shackle a man in the bondage of the nakedness mindset and the bondage of the sin nature.
b. Condemnation causes a man to linger on an irrepressible sense of judgment, guilt, shame, and fear.
c. Both statements summarize the truth about condemnation.

The more we grow spiritually, the more God-conscious we become. The more God-conscious we become the more we experience conviction, increasing our capacity to make God-honoring, covenant-keeping choices. When we fail to do so, we are immediately faced with a choice.

The choices following a transgression for a clothed man include:

1. The choice of conviction
2. The choice of condemnation
3. Both choices are faced following a transgression

Which choice do you choose most often when you experience a transgression? Explain why.

____
____
____
____

Conviction should not lead to condemnation. Place the right word in the descriptions below.
________________________ is our enemy, our adversary, and a constant agitator, deceiver, and tempter, trying to convince us that we are still naked.
________________________ is our companion and advocate; a very present help; a constant counselor of salvation's benefits, righteousness and reminder that we are clothed with Christ.

God makes a distinction between a man who is convicted and a man who is condemned. The lives of two disciples: Peter and Judas provide biblical evidence of this distinction. Which disciple was convicted and which disciple was condemned?

1. Peter: Convicted / Condemned
2. Judas: Convicted / Condemned

Matthew 12:34,37

Explain the distinction between the two disciples. (p. 70-73)
Peter:

____

____

____

____

Matthew 26:14-16; John 6:70

Judas:

____

____

____

____

What actions did Peter take to get to Jesus in order to confess his transgressions? (p. 73)

____

____

____

____

Taking lessons from Peter's experience, what actions should men take following a transgression?

____

____

____

____

After Jesus' crucifixion, the disciples went fishing. Oddly enough, Peter was naked in the boat while they were fishing. When Jesus called out to them from the shore, it was John who recognized the

Notes:

voice was that of Jesus. John had to tell Peter who it was calling out to them.

The lesson here is, a naked man cannot recognize the voice of Jesus. A clothed man has to make it known to him. Peter was spiritually clothed but had a naked mindset due to [condemnation/conviction]. As clothed men, we must never allow the weight of our conviction to lead to condemnation.

What did God say to you in Chapter 6?

____

____

____

____

Write what you want to say to God based on what you have heard him say to you.

Heavenly Father:

____

____

____

____

Chapter 7

The State of Depravity

Then the Lord saw the wickedness of man was great upon the earth and that every imagination of the thoughts of his heart was only evil continually. Genesis 6:5

God blessed them and said, "Be fruitful and increase in number and fill the water in the seas, and let the birds increase on the earth." ***Gen. 1:22***

God blessed them and said to them, "Be fruitful and increase in number; fill the earth and subdue it. Rule over the fish in the sea and the birds in the sky and over every living creature that moves on the ground." ***Gen. 1:28***

7Then the Lord God formed a man[a] from the dust of the ground and breathed into his nostrils the breath of life, and the man became a living being. 8 Now the Lord God had planted a garden in the east, in Eden; and there he put the man he had formed. ***Gen. 2:7-8***

God made man in his own image and according to his likeness. Man was given authority to rule over everything in the earth. As the Creator, God's first act towards man was to bless them and empower them to have authority over everything he created and to be successful (vv.22, 28)

God's first recorded words to man were, "Be fruitful and multiply, and fill the earth, and subdue it; and rule over the fish of the seas and over the birds in the sky and over every living thing that moves on the earth." God established expectations. He also provided instruction for food and for everything that moves on the earth.

1. As the Creator, God's first act towards man was to (Choose the best answer). (p. 75)

   a. Bless them and empower them to have authority over everything he created
   b. Empower them to be successful
   c. Establish expectations
   d. All the above

2. In the blank provided, write the chapter and verse where each scripture below is found in the Bible. (p. 75)

   a. "The Lord God formed man of the dust from the ground, and breathed into his nostrils the breath of life, and man became a living being." ______________________
   b. "The Lord God planted a garden and there he placed the man whom he formed." ______________________

3. What four (4) things did the Lord create and provide in order to ensure Adam fulfilled his purpose? (pp.75-76)

   a. The Lord God ________________________________
   b. The Lord God ________________________________
   c. The Lord provided ____________________________
   d. The Lord took the man __________________________

Notes:

4. Which of the following statements is true? (Circle the correct answer)

   a. Death occurred when Adam ate—not when Eve ate.
   b. Both of them did not die.

5. Which is true regarding zombies as compared to a man who is spiritually dead?

   a. A spiritually dead man is like a zombie, he cannot be reasoned with or placated.
   b. No matter how much of the world he takes in, he cannot be satisfied.
   c. A is true
   d. Both A and B are correct.

6. Which are the effects of a man who has had too much red wine? (Circle the correct answer)

a. His heart begins to conjure up wonderful fantasies
b. When he lies down, it is as if he is lying in the midst of the sea upon a mat
c. When his head clears from the stupor of his hangover, he will repeat the same pattern all over again
d. All but A are correct

7. The longings of a spiritually dead man are continuous attempts to quench an appetite for which of the following: (p. 77)

   a. The lust of the flesh
   b. The lust of the eyes
   c. The pride of life
   d. All the above

Notes:

Choose the word from the list below to complete the sentences:

1. Craving
2. Possessions
3. Overwhelming
4. Sexual desire
5. Appetite
6. passionate

8. In the text we read that lust is a __________, __________ desire or __________ for things such as power, prestige, money, and other ______________. (p. 78)

   The most common use of the word "lust" is in the context of intense __________ or __________; or uncontrolled, illicit ______________.

Lust Originates in the Heart

9. God wants a man to be rich, but according to his plan and purpose. In addition, God wants a man to have prestige, but according to his plan and for his glory. Which of the following are true regarding what God does not want for us?

   a. God does not want a man to be sexually depraved
   b. God does not want a man to be broke
   c. God does not want a man to be insignificant.
   d. All of the above

10. Apart from a relationship with God, a man's motives are driven by (fill in the blank) p. 79

    - Self- ____________
    - Self- ____________
    - Self- ____________

11. A naked man's motives are driven by sensuality—lust of the

flesh, lust of the eyes and the pride of life; not spirituality—love, joy, peace, patience, kindness, gentleness, faithfulness, goodness and self-control. Complete the following statements:

a. __________ drives the personality of a naked man
b. __________ drives the personality of a clothed man

Of the two conditions, are you more sensually motivated or spiritually motivated? Explain your answer.

____

____

____

____

The Lust of the Flesh

12. The seventeen works of the flesh are described in Galatians 5:19-21. Below, please name 10 of them: (Define each using at least four words to describe each).

1. Adultery:

____

2. Fornication:

____

3. Uncleanness:

____

4. Lasciviousness:

____

5. Idolatry:

____

Notes:

Notes:

6. Witchcraft:

____

7. Hatred:

____

8. Variance:

____

9. Emulations:

____

10. Wrath:

____

13. Notice the top four matters of lust of the flesh are related to sex. Complete the following sentence. (p. 84)

    a. __________ outside of God's plan and purpose always leaves a man __________.

14. Since procreation is a spiritual act between carnal beings, God intended it to occur only in the institution of holy matrimony— __________. Fill in the blanks.

    a. As such, since God made sex for procreation, he only intended it to be between a __________ and a __________.

15. Often times the things we see stir up cravings and imaginations that are far from our minds. (Please circle the best answer):

    a. Lusts of the eyes are the unintentional or the deliberate efforts to seek out those things which stimulate thoughts, imaginations, and fantasies for sensual gratification.
    b. Unrestrained episodes of lust of the eyes eventually go beyond thoughts, imaginations, and fantasies and lead to physical acts of sin.

c. We have enough challenges wrestling with memories of the wild and crazy things we did in our wilderness years before we were saved.
d. All of the above.

16. When a man's eyes lack spiritual discipline it will lead him to lust for __________, lust for other __________, covetousness, idolatry and all kinds of __________ and __________. Fill in the blanks. (p. 87)

a. The scriptures encourage us to guard our heart, for out of it flows the __________.
b. Men should be even more __________ to guard their eyes, for they are the entry point to a man's soul which stores up the things that come out of __________.

17. Which of the following statements are true of the clothed man and the naked man? Underline the correct answer. (p. 87)

a. Convicted by even the thought of the visual transgression and does not want it to go any further. Clothed Man / Naked Man
b. Does not consider the consequences. In some cases, he actually does but is willing to take the risks. Clothed Man / Naked Man

18. David grew strong in the Lord after his transgression with Bathsheba. True or False? (p. 87)

a. Rather than being intentional in seeking opportunities to lust, clothed men do everything they can to avoid it. True / False

19. Which of the following are true concerning Pride? Circle which apply.

a. Serving self for the purpose of satisfying egotistic motives and ambitions is the pride of life.

1 Have mercy on me, O God, according to your unfailing love; according to your great compassion blot out my transgressions.
2 Wash away all my iniquity and cleanse me from my sin. 3 For I know my transgressions, and my sin is always before me. 4 Against you, you only, have I sinned and done what is evil in your sight; so you are right in your verdict and justified when you judge. 5 Surely I was sinful at birth, sinful from the time my mother conceived me. 6 Yet you desired faithfulness even in the womb; you taught me wisdom in that secret place. 7 Cleanse me with hyssop, and I will be clean; wash me, and I will be whiter than snow. 8 Let me hear joy and gladness; let the bones you have crushed rejoice. 9 Hide your face from my sins and blot out all my iniquity. 10 Create in me a pure heart, O God, and renew a steadfast spirit within me. ***Psalm 51***

Notes:

b. Pride leads to condemnation of the devil.
c. Some men are so driven by power, influence, and money they will do almost anything to get it.
d. Addiction to prestige has caused men to get involved in activities such as financial fraud, drug dealing and high stakes gambling.
e. All of the above

20. God's covenant is filled with exceedingly great and precious promises which confirm his desire for sons of God to have a prestigious and prosperous life for his glory, not for our self-aggrandizement (ambition). Complete the Scripture by filling in the blanks:

Jeremiah 29:11:"I know the __________ I have for you says the Lord; __________ to __________ you, not to __________ you; to give you a __________ and a __________."

21. God's plan for a man includes prospering him in every area of his life. It is his will that his sons be renown in the earth, set apart, and distinguished from other men. His aspirations for his sons include making our name great (Genesis 12:2). His covenant includes:

a. Making us the head and not the tail, above only and not beneath. True / False

22. Which of the following are not true? Circle the correct answer(s). (p. 89)

a. God only has a plan for our prestige
b. God has a process whereby he develops a man to a level of humility, maturity, and spirituality
c. God has a track record of bringing men from obscurity to prominence
d. God's succession plan for Daniel took him from a Jewish slave to a governor of one of the provinces
e. A
f. C and A

23. God has a motive for taking us through trials and tribulations as he works his plan of prestige in our lives. His motive is that when we arrive at our place of destiny, we do not forget that it is he who has brought us through the wilderness into our land of material prosperity and public prominence. Complete the scripture below: Deuteronomy 8:17-18

a. "And thou say in thine heart, my power and the might of mine hand hath gotten me this wealth. But thou shalt remember the Lord thy God: for it is he that giveth thee power to get wealth, that He:

____

____

____

____

You may say to yourself, "My power and the strength of my hands have produced this wealth for me." 18 But remember the Lord your God, for it is he who gives you the ability to produce wealth, and so confirms his covenant, which he swore to your ancestors, as it is today. ***Deut. 8:17-18***

24. God desires for us to have wealth, but he wants us to gain it according to his plan and his way. According to his word, he wants us to have enough money to: Circle the correct answer(s). Pay tithes and give offerings Malachi 3:8-10

a. Have all sufficiency to give on every occasion
b. Lend to many nations and not have to borrow
c. Have wealth and riches in our house
d. Leave an inheritance to his children's children
e. All but B
f. All of the above

2 Corinth. 9:8

Deut. 28:12

Psalm 112:3

Proverbs 13:22

25. A son of the Most High God should not be barely making it from paycheck to paycheck, taking out payday loans, title pawn loans, and borrowing money from his neighbors and friends to feed his family. This is the lifestyle of: (Circle the correct answer)

a. Clothed man
b. Naked man

26. According to the text, Clothed men should not have to experience foreclosure, car repossession, and bankruptcy. The Word of God in Proverbs 10:22 declares: (Complete the scripture by filling in the missing word.)

a. The __________ of the Lord makes one rich, and he adds no sorrow with it.

20 So he got up and went to his father. "But while he was still a long way off, his father saw him and was filled with compassion for him; he ran to his son, threw his arms around him and kissed him.

21 "The son said to him, 'Father, I have sinned against heaven and against you. I am no longer worthy to be called your son.'

22 "But the father said to his servants, 'Quick! Bring the best robe and put it on him. Put a ring on his finger and sandals on his feet.
Luke 15:20-22

27. Lust of the flesh, lust of the eyes, and the pride of life have caused and continues to cause men to fall short of being all God has called us to be. Circle the correct answer: A lifestyle of lust and pride is the lifestyle of:

a. A naked man
b. A clothed man

28. The serpent still wants to deceive and deprive us of the presence of God. God has restored ancient Eden. The Kingdom of God is here. However, there is a dress code, a prerequisite for entering into Kingdom ecstasy. We must be clothed with Christ (Galatians 3:27). (Which of the following are true?): Circle the correct answer. (p. 93)

a. For men who are still naked, the serpent is working hard to keep them naked in order to keep them out.
b. To those who are clothed, he is working diligently to convince them they are still naked in order that they would not walk in their inheritance as kingdom men.
c. B is True
d. Neither are True
e. Both A and B are True

29. Depravation (immorality) has the tendency to keep a man in the hog pen trying to figure out a solution to the mess that he has made. The grace of God leads a depraved man to repentance. (pp. 94-96)

a. The above statements best describe which biblical character?

_______________________.

30. According to Colossians 3:12-14 (Fill in the blank):

a. The basic, all-purpose garment of a Clothed Man is _____.

What did God say to you in Chapter 7?

____

____

____

____

Write what you want to say to God based on what you have heard him say to you.

Heavenly Father:

____

____

____

____

12 Therefore, as God's chosen people, holy and dearly loved, clothe yourselves with compassion, kindness, humility, gentleness and patience. 13 Bear with each other and forgive one another if any of you has a grievance against someone. Forgive as the Lord forgave you. 14 And over all these virtues put on love, which binds them all together in perfect unity. **Colossians 3:12-14**

Chapter 8

Lead Us Not Into Temptation

Let no man say when he is tempted, I am tempted of God: for God cannot be tempted with evil, neither tempteth he any man: But every man is tempted, when he is drawn away of his own lust and enticed. Then when lust hath conceived, it bringeth forth death. James 1:13-15

Notes:

Every man is tempted with lust of the flesh, lust of the eyes and with pride. Each of us have our __________________ and our __________________ . We all have repressed sensations etched in our flesh from the days before we committed our lives to Christ. Many of us are challenged with how long to look at a beautiful woman without allowing lust to be __________________ , or how long to look in awe at certain material possessions of others without being __________________. Additionally, there are those among our ranks who wrestle with aspirations of success and achievement whose motive is not for the glory of God but to glorify self. In spite of these truths, we should not be __________________. Jesus was tempted at all points as we are, yet without sin (Hebrews 4:15). Because Jesus was __________________ over temptation, we too have the victory.

Choose the word from the list below to complete the sentences:

a. Pride
b. Eyes
c. Flesh

1. Every man is tempted with lust of the flesh, lust of the _______, and with ___________. There are those among our ranks who wrestle with aspirations of success and achievement whose motives is not for the glory of God but to glorify self.

Circle the correct answer.

a. Jesus was tempted at all points as we are, yet without sin. True / False
b. Because Jesus was victorious over temptation, does not always mean that we have the victory as well. True / False

Choose the word from the list below to complete the sentences:

a. Linger (used twice)
b. Conception
c. Caught up

d. Drawn away
e. Give place
f. Dwell
g. Lust

2. We fall when we allow ourselves to be __________ __________, __________ __________ in the moment, and ________________ in the thought processes that lead to the __________ of lust. (p. 98)

   a. If we ________ ________, ________, ________, permit the opportunity for prolonged exposure to our vulnerabilities and weaknesses, we are at the risk of being drawn away into our own __________.

3. The tendencies, ways, and habits of our flesh that the "old man" was accustomed to during our undisciplined wilderness years is also known as: (Circle the correct answer)

   a. Misgivings
   b. Lusts
   c. Weaknesses
   d. All of the above

4. The enemy deliberately provokes us with people, places, and things that are strategically engineered to make us fall into temptation because: Circle the best answer:

   a. He knows we can be enticed
   b. He knows the specific misgivings we have wrestled with
   c. He knows when we are at our weakest
   d. All of the above

5. Temptation initiated the sequence of events in the human spirit which led to Adam's transgression. Which of the statements below is true regarding the clothed man? (Circle the correct answer):

   a. The clothed man seeks the purpose and promises of God

Notes:

The acts of the flesh are obvious: sexual immorality, impurity and debauchery; 20 idolatry and witchcraft; hatred, discord, jealousy, fits of rage, selfish ambition, dissensions, factions 21 and envy; drunkenness, orgies, and the like. I warn you, as I did before, that those who live like this will not inherit the kingdom of God. ***Gal. 5:19-21***

b. The clothed man faces temptation
c. Both A & B

6. Temptation feeds the thoughts and imaginations of the human spirit continuously. What two things do we consistently wonder when faced with temptation?

   (Circle the correct answer found in the text)

   a. "What if ?" - Or, "I wonder what it would be like to...?"
   b. "I wonder did anyone see me? - Or, What if I just make this the last time?
   c. Both A and B

7. Righteous men should not fear temptation, though it is easier said than done. When considering all seventeen works of the flesh studied in Galatians 5, men are tested relentlessly in some way, shape, or form to transgress in many of them. (p. 99)

(Complete the sentences below which further describe the difference between the mindset of the clothed man and the naked man. Fill in the blanks):

a. A ____________ man has resigned to the sinful nature and is content being __________.
b. A ____________ man diligently fights, and is never satisfied with transgression (wrongdoing).

8. A clothed man's strength is in the Lord. He overcomes the valleys of temptation and with each victory, he grows stronger and stronger as he diligently seeks and abides in the Lord his God.

What does Psalm 84:5-7 say to support this position? (Quote the entire scripture).

____

____

____

____

9. The people of Sodom and Gomorrah were condemned to destruction by being reduced to ashes.

Why did God make an example for future reference? Complete the sentence below. Fill in the blanks:

a. God made an example out of them to

____

____

10. 2 Peter 2:9 – Although Sodom and Gomorrah were destroyed, Lot was not harmed – why? (p. 100) Complete the scripture verse by filling in the blank spaces:

a. The Lord knows how to rescue the ________________ godly out of ________________, and to reserve the ______________ unto the Day of Judgment.

11. The word of God says in James 1:13; "Because it is God who delivers from temptation, no man can say that he is tempted of God."

James 1:14-15, says: (Fill in the blanks to complete the scripture):

a. "But every man is tempted,

____

____

_____________ and enticed. Then when ___________ hath conceived, it bringeth forth __________: and __________ it is finished, bringeth forth __________"

12. Oh, what treasures we forfeit when we give in to temptation.

For if God did not spare angels when they sinned, but sent them to hell,[a] putting them in chains of darkness[b] to be held for judgment; 5 if he did not spare the ancient world when he brought the flood on its ungodly people, but protected Noah, a preacher of righteousness, and seven others; 6 if he condemned the cities of Sodom and Gomorrah by burning them to ashes, and made them an example of what is going to happen to the ungodly; 7 and if he rescued Lot, a righteous man, who was distressed by the depraved conduct of the lawless 8 (for that righteous man, living among them day after day, was tormented in his righteous soul by the lawless deeds he saw and heard)— 9 if this is so, then the Lord knows how to rescue the godly from trials and to hold the unrighteous for punishment on the day of judgment. ***2 Peters 2:4-9***

No temptation[a] has overtaken you except what is common to mankind. And God is faithful; he will not let you be tempted[b] beyond what you can bear. But when you are tempted,[c] he will also provide a way out so that you can endure it. **1 Corith. 10:13**

Complete the scripture below by filling in the blanks.

James 1:12
"Blessed is the man that endures __________; for when he is tried, he shall receive the __________ of __________ which the Lord hath __________ __________ __________ __________ which the Lord hath promised to them that __________ him."

13. How does God work His "good pleasure" in the life of a clothed man prior to that man committing a transgression (wrongdoing)? Select the correct answer below: (p. 102)

    a. Through that man's conscious
    b. Through that man's good deeds
    c. Through the Holy Spirit

The Escape Route

1 Corinthians 10:13 says God always provides an escape route when we are faced with temptation. Because he always does, when a man chooses to transgress, is he then under condemnation? Yes / No

Condemnation is never the appropriate response for a clothed man. True / False

14. Observe the following statements and identify whether they are True or False. (p. 103) Circle the correct answer.

    a. Conviction is God at work in us, coaching us to choose according to his good pleasure. True / False
    b. When we fail and yield, neither conviction, nor condemnation brings us to the prayer of forgiveness and repentance. True / False

What did God say to you in Chapter 8?

____

____

Write what you want to say to God based on what you have heard him say to you.

Heavenly Father:

Notes:

Chapter 9

The Wrestling Match

For we wrestle not against flesh and blood, but against principalities, against powers, against the rulers of the darkness of this world, against spiritual wickedness in high places. Ephesians 6:12

Then Jesus was led by the Spirit into the wilderness to be tempted[a] by the devil. ***Matthew 4:1***

For we do not have a high priest who is unable to empathize with our weaknesses, but we have one who has been tempted in every way, just as we are—yet he did not sin. ***Hebrews 4:15***

Temptation in and of itself is not sin. Jesus was "in all points tempted as we are, yet without sin." (Hebrews 4:15) Jesus was tempted by the devil in the wilderness with opportunities which correlate to all three categories of carnal challenge: the lust of the flesh, the lust of the eyes, and the pride of life. Having heard the proposals of Satan for his consideration, Jesus cancelled each with scripture. Considering a matter does not constitute a transgression. When we cancel it out with scripture and prayer, the temptation does not progress to a sinful act. In other words, when considering the seven steps of temptation, we can be tempted, drawn away, lust, and enticed. We can draw strength through conviction to speak scripture to our situation and pray, but never reach the point of yielding. However, as clothed men, righteous men, godly men, and good men we are in a constant wrestling match vacillating between the naked mentality and the clothed mentality; between conviction and condemnation.

1. According to Ephesians 6:12, who are our opponents in the wrestling match?

____

____

____

____

2. Who did Paul say was the thorn in his flesh?

____

____

____

____

3. What is the specific job description of the messenger of Satan?

____

____

____

____

4. What is a quintessential trait for the man who would be a transformer for the kingdom of God? (p. 109)

____

____

Our opponents in the wrestling match are principalities, powers, rulers of darkness of this world, spiitual wickedness in high places. The thorn in the flesh is the messenger of Satan. His job description is to buffet and betray the quintessential trait of the man who would be a transformer in the kingdom of God is humility.

5. Should a Christian live in condemnation or with conviction? Why did God allow the "thorn in the flesh"? Explain.

6. What did God say to Paul when he prayed to remove the thorn in his flesh?

The Issue of Infirmities

7. Did Paul have many infirmities? Yes or no? __________

8. How many infirmities are identified in Galatians 5:19-21?

a. one
b. eight
c. seventeen

Case Study: Samson—A Man of God with Many Infirmities

9. Was Samson a man of infirmities? Why or why not?

or because of these surpassingly great revelations. Therefore, in order to keep me from becoming conceited, I was given a thorn in my flesh, a messenger of Satan, to torment me. 8 Three times I pleaded with the Lord to take it away from me. 9 But he said to me, "My grace is sufficient for you, for my power is made perfect in weakness." Therefore I will boast all the more gladly about my weaknesses, so that Christ's power may rest on me.
2 Corith. 12:7-9

It was good for me to be afflicted so that I might learn your decrees.
Psalm 119:71

Judges

Notes:

10. Lessons learned from the life of Samson: (pp. 116-117)

10. *Choose the word from the list below to complete the sentences:*

1. infirmities
2. releases
3. woman
4. intimated
5. persists
6. anointing
7. character
8. temptation
9. depravity

a. Satan is not __________ by your __________ if he has control of your __________.

b. Samson's __________ and __________ kept taking him back to the same kind of __________.

c. When a clothed man __________ in dabbling in his __________ and does not put up a good fight of faith with temptation, God __________ him to his own demise.

What did God say to you in Chapter 9?

____

____

____

____

Write what you want to say to God based on what you have heard him say to you.

Heavenly Father:

____

____

____

____

Chapter 10

Work Out Your Soul Salvation

Wherefore, my beloved, as ye have always obeyed, not as in my presence only, but now much more in my absence, work out your own soul salvation with fear and trembling.
Philippians 2:12

2 Peter 1:2-10

To work out your soul salvation is to put into practice God's saving work in our lives. To work at establishing a lifestyle of order and discipline, aligned with the precepts, values and principles of the Word of God. "With fear and trembling", speaks to the intensity of our reverence toward our God and our staunch determination to do those things that are pleasing in his sight. The Message Bible translation says it this way, "Be energetic in your life of salvation, reverent and sensitive before God." Philippians 2:12

1. How do we work out our soul's salvation?

   a. We put into practice God's saving work in our lives.
   b. We establish a lifestyle of order and discipline aligned with the precepts, values, and principles of the word of God.
   c. Have a steady-state lifestyle of "walking in the Spirit".
   d. All the above.

2. What type of lifestyle should be displayed as a clothed man?

____

____

____

____

Until we all reach unity in the faith and in the knowledge of the Son of God and become mature, attaining to the whole measure of the fullness of Christ. ***Eph. 4:13***

3. In order for God to be at work in us to will and to do according to his good pleasure (Philippians 2:13) the two things a man must do is: (p. 119)

   a. Be a ______________________________.
   b. Have a ______________________________.

For it is God who works in you to will and to act in order to fulfill his good purpose. ***Phil. 2:13***

When a man works out physically, his body becomes the evidence of the diligent efforts he has demonstrated over a period of time. In the spiritual sense, a clothed man must work out [his soul salvation] in order that: (p. 120)

   a. We will increase more and more in spiritual evidence that we are sons of God.

b. We will increase more and more in physical evidence that we are sons of God.
c. We will increase more and more in material evidence that we are sons of God.
d. All the above

4. What is the motivation of the clothed man's work out?

a. The prize of the high calling of God
b. Greater rewards and greater purposes for God's elect
c. The joy of redemption when he fails short
d. Spiritual attributes of a son of God
e. All are motivating factors for a clothed man's work out.

We Have a Coach

5. Just as athletes have coaches to provide resources to develop athletes to maximum potential, God also provide resources to develop clothed men to maximum potential. List the resources God provide. (pp. 122-123)

____
____
____
____

The Diligence of the Clothed Man

Diligently working out our soul salvation simply explains the spiritual work ethic of a man who has made up his mind that he is going after all that God has promised.

6. Clothed men must be as diligent as professional athletes to attain all Go has promised. Fill in the blanks regarding the four characteristics of a diligent clothed man. (p. 124)

Do you not know that in a race all the runners run, but only one gets the prize? Run in such a way as to get the prize. 25 Everyone who competes in the games goes into strict training. They do it to get a crown that will not last, but we do it to get a crown that will last forever. 26 Therefore I do not run like someone running aimlessly; I do not fight like a boxer beating the air. 27 No, I strike a blow to my body and make it my slave so that after I have preached to others, I myself will not be disqualified for the prize. ***1 Corinth. 9:24-27***

Notes:

Choose the word from the list below to complete the sentences:

1. Persevering
2. Hardworking
3. Assignments
4. Constant
5. Persistent
6. Attentive
7. Careful

a. __________ and __________ in their efforts to accomplish what has been undertaken

b. __________ and __________ in the disciplines necessary to achieve their destiny

c. __________ and industrious

d. __________ and steady in all their decisions, __________ through difficult __________

7. List six activities commonly associated with a commitment to spiritual work outs. (pp. 124-125)

____

____

____

____

What did God say to you in Chapter 10?

____

____

____

____

Write what you want to say to God based upon what you have heard him say to you.

Heavenly Father:

____

____

____

____

Chapter 11

The Disciplined Life of a Clothed Man

But if the Spirit of him who raised up Jesus from the dead dwell in you, he that raised Christ shall quicken your mortal bodies by his Spirit that dwells in you. Romans 8:11

Yet, before the twins were born or had done anything good or bad—in order that God's purpose in election might stand. **Romans 9:11**

For it is God who works in you to will and to act in order to fulfill his good purpose. **Phil. 2:13**

Romans 8:1-11

Walking in the Spirit

The Spirit of God dwells in a clothed man. It is not the works of the law that sustains him spiritually. It is the Holy Spirit within the clothed man that sustains him spiritually. God the Holy Spirit does the work (Romans 9:11; Philippians 2:13). We do not have the capacity in our carnal condition to make ourselves righteous. If we did, there would have been no need for Jesus to come.

1. The Holy Spirit in a clothed man (fill in the blanks).

   a. __________ us spiritually
   b. Does the __________ in us
   c. __________ us righteous

2. Circle the word which best fits. The Spirit of God dwells in a clothed / naked man.

The Work of the Holy Spirit

1. Which of the following are descriptions of what it means to "walk in the Spirit"? (p. 130)

   a. Continuous steady-state process
   b. Moving forward step by step
   c. Falling down and getting back up again
   d. Relentlessly pursuing God's destiny
   e. All are descriptions of "walking in the Spirit".

"Walking in the Spirit" is a continuous steady-state of moving forward step by step toward the purpose and calling of God—falling down, getting back up again, relentlessly pursuing a God ordained Kingdom destiny.

2. Which of the following are descriptions of what it means to be "walking in the flesh"? (p. 130)

   a. Continuous steady-state process

b. Moving forward step by step
c. Toward lust of the flesh, lust of the eyes and the pride of life
d. Relentlessly pursuing carnal cravings
e. All are descriptions of "walking in the flesh".

"Walking in the flesh" is a continuous steady-state of moving forward step by step toward the lust of the flesh, the lust of the eyes and the pride of life—falling down, getting back up again, relentlessly pursuing carnal cravings which ultimately lead to destruction.

3. Mind things of the flesh, carnally minded, enmity with God, spiritually dead, self is helper are all related to: (p. 131)

   a. Walking in the Spirit
   b. Walking in the Flesh
   c. Both a and b are correct

4. Mind things of the Spirit, spiritually minded, reconciled to God, spiritually alive, Spirit as helper are all related to: (p. 131)

   a. Walking in the Spirit
   b. Walking in the Flesh
   c. Both a and b are correct

5. Walking in the Spirit is manifested through a disposition of: (p. 131)

   a. Submitting our will to the Lordship of Christ
   b. Accepting the challenge of sufferings associated with growth
   c. Following Christ day to day
   d. All the above

6. The Steps of overcoming the stronghold of condemnation for a clothed man are: (p. 132)

Choose the word from the list below to complete the sentences:

   a. Sensitivity

Then he said to them all: "Whoever wants to be my disciple must deny themselves and take up their cross daily and follow me. ***Luke 9:23***

If you fully obey the Lord your God and carefully follow all his commands I give you today, the Lord your God will set you high above all the nations on earth. ***Deut. 28:1***

Therefore, I urge you, brothers and sisters, in view of God's mercy, to offer your bodies as a living sacrifice, holy and pleasing to God—this is your true and proper worship. 2 Do not conform to the pattern of this world, but be transformed by the renewing of your mind. Then you will be able to test and approve what God's will is—his good, pleasing and perfect will. ***Romans 12:1-2***

Blessed is the one who does not walk in step with the wicked or stand in the way that sinners take or sit in the company of mockers, 2 but whose delight is in the law of the Lord, and who meditates on his law day and night. 3 That person is like a tree planted by streams of water,which yields its fruit in season and whose leaf does not wither—whatever they do prospers. **Psalm 1:1-3**

Psalm 128

b. God
c. Spending
d. Fasting
e. Awareness
f. Clothed men
g. spirit-man
h. Prayer
i. All day long

Step 1:	__________ quiet time
Step 2:	__________ and __________
Step 3:	Daily __________ on the Word of God
Step 4:	Wholesome relationships with __________ and __________
Step 5:	__________ to others

7. Daily quiet time is all about _______________ time with _________________.

8. A clothed man should pray one time a day-- ____________.

9. A combination of __________ and __________ invokes a greater level of spiritual __________, power and __________ to the guidance of the Holy Spirit. (p. 136)

10. As __________ __________ men we must establish a way of life where we are consistent in feeding our spirit-man of God's word. (p. 137)

11. Sermons on Sunday, Bible study on Wednesday, and occasional television messages are all the nourishment a man need to maximize spiritual virtue. True / False

12. One of the greatest resources of conquest in overcoming the stronghold of condemnation for a clothed man is:

a. His career

b. His hobbies
c. His family
d. His pastor

13. Do you need an accountability partner? Why or why not?

____
____
____
____

14. Who would make a great accountability partner for you? Why?

____
____
____
____

What did God say to you in Chapter 11?

____
____
____
____

15. According to Joshua 1:7-8 and Psalm 1:1-3, what are the promises God has made to the man who meditates on his Word day and night?

a. ____________________
b. ____________________
c. ____________________
d. ____________________

"Be strong and very courageous. Be careful to obey all the law my servant Moses gave you; do not turn from it to the right or to the left, that you may be successful wherever you go. 8 Keep this Book of the Law always on your lips; meditate on it day and night, so that you may be careful to do everything written in it. Then you will be prosperous and successful. ***Joshua 1:7-8***

Notes:

Write what you want to say to God based upon what you have heard him say to you.

Heavenly Father:

Chapter 12

A Spirit-Filled Virtuous Life

Grace and peace be multiplied unto you through the knowledge of God, and of Jesus our Lord, according as his divine power hath given us all things that pertain to life and godliness, through the knowledge of him that hath called us to glory and virtue; whereby are given unto us exceeding great and precious promises: that by these ye might be partakers of the divine nature, having escaped the corruption that is in the world through lust. And by all this, add to your faith virtue. 2 Peter 1:2-5

As you know, it was because of an illness that I first preached the gospel to you...
Gal. 4:13

It is God's desire that as clothed men, we are filled with all the fullness of God, unto the fullness of the measure and stature of Christ (Galatians 4:13). Consistently exercising the disciplines of a clothed man sustains us at our spiritual peak.

1. What is the compelling evidence of a lifestyle of a clothed man? Explain. (p. 143)

____

____

____

____

According to *II Peter 1:2-3, God has given us all things that pertain to life and godliness. Through the knowledge of him that hath called us to glory and virtue.* A spirit-filled life is a life manifesting God's glory and virtue. The lifestyle of a clothed man is one that in all roles, relationships and responsibilities reveals compelling evidence that he is a son of God. In other words, people can look at his life and see that all the promises of God are true because he is living proof.

Called to Glory

The glory of God in clothed men is the expressions of the attributes of God manifested in spiritual gifts and spiritual fruit.

The definitions of glory in the Greek include which of the following:

a. Very apparent
b. Dignity
c. Honor
d. Praise
e. Apprehended
f. All are definitions of glory

How to recognize God's Glory.

2. What are the fruits of the spirit? (p. 144) List.

____

____

____

____

3. Record the definition of virtue in the space provided below. (p. 145)

___

___

___

___

Of the two words "glory" and "virtue" the statements below are most descriptive of which?

a. The physical and spiritual resources essential to living victoriously, in all things that pertain to life and godliness. Glory / Virtue
b. The divine order that energizes and gives meaning purpose, stamina and focus to our existence as men. Glory / Virtue

4. What did Smith Wigglesworth say about virtue? Explain (p. 146)

___

___

___

___

5. What is the definition of faith? (p. 149)

___

___

___

___

Complete this sentence. (p. 149)

__________ and __________ sustains our victory over condemnation and conviction.

___

___

___

___

At once Jesus realized that power had gone out from him. He turned around in the crowd and asked, "Who touched my clothes?" ***Mark 5:30***

And the people all tried to touch him, because power was coming from him and healing them all. ***Luke 6:19***

But Jesus said, "Someone touched me; I know that power has gone out from me." ***Luke 8:46***

Now faith is confidence in what we hope for and assurance about what we do not see. ***Hebrews 11:1***

For this very reason, make every effort to add to your faith goodness; and to goodness, knowledge... ***2 Peter 1:5***

A man cannot walk in a state of deprivation when he is full of faith and virtue. He knows that "the promises of God in him are yea, and in him, Amen unto the glory of God by us!"(II Corinthians 1:20). He knows emphatically that God is his source and that nothing that he needs will be denied of the Father. When our virtue is consistently low, we beg and plead to our Father for what we need. When our virtue is full we come before him boldly and confidently with our petitions. (p. 150)

Faith, glory and virtue are the present tense of divine power which causes us to act and talk as if the things that we believe God for has already occurred. (p.150)

What does virtue mean to you? Explain.

What is the definition of virtue in the Hebrew translation?

What did God say to you in Chapter 12?

Write what you want to say to God based upon what you have heard him say to you.

Heavenly Father:

Chapter 13

We Have Overcome the Stronghold of Condemnation

There is therefore now no condemnation to those who are in Christ Jesus, who do not walk according to the flesh, but according to the Spirit. Romans 8:1

*They will turn their ears away from the truth and turn aside to myths. 5 But you, keep your head in all situations, endure hardship, do the work of an evangelist, discharge all the duties of your minist*ry. ***2 Tim. 4:4-5***

"I have told you these things, so that in me you may have peace. In this world you will have trouble. But take heart! I have overcome the world." ***John 16:33***

Then I heard a loud voice in heaven say: "Now have come the salvation and the power and the kingdom of our God, and the authority of his Messiah. For the accuser of our brothers and sisters, who accuses them before our God day and night, has been hurled down. 11 They triumphed over him by the blood of the Lamb and by the word of their testimony; they did not love their lives so much as to shrink from death. ***Rev. 12:10-11***

In spite of The Cross—and everything we know about The Blood of Jesus, we have been treating sin as an incurable disease. Condemnation constantly renews this mindset. Jesus came to cure the world from its sin condition. He accomplished what he came here to do! "It is finished!!!"

1. Why is condemnation considered a stronghold? (p. 153) Explain.

____

____

____

____

Christ overcoming gives us glory and virtue that we too shall overcome. Why?

____

____

____

____

2. Explain Romans 8:1-6 in your own words?

____

____

____

____

3. Rejecting Jesus after being enlightened of him is condemnation. It is a conscious choice to choose darkness over light. True / False

4. Christ gives us ________________ over condemnation.

   a. success
   b. victory
   c. peace
   d. guilt

5. When a __________ man overcomes it brings salvation to his entire household.

6. Clothed men serving from the heart are predominately________ (p. 156)

7. Naked, self-serving men are predominately __________.

8. Being transformed in the renewing of our minds means:

a. we are redeemed
b. we are sinners
c. we are not righteous
d. we are not deprived
e. both a & d

9. Which set of words match the sentences below?

The __________ , love, __________, the works of the __________ and the pleasures of __________ more than __________.

The __________, love, the works of the __________ and the pleasures of __________ and therefore walk in the light.

a. Clothed, spirit, righteous, light
b. Naked, darkness, flesh, sin

What did God say to you in Chapter 13?

____

____

____

____

Write what you want to say to God based upon what you have heard him say to you.

____

____

____

____

He told us how he had seen an angel appear in his house and say, 'Send to Joppa for Simon who is called Peter. 14 He will bring you a message through which you and all your household will be saved.' ***Acts 11:13-14***

Therefore, there is now no condemnation for those who are in Christ Jesus... ***Romans 8:1***

Notes:

Heavenly Father:

References

Eerdmans, W. B., (2000)Eerdmans Dictionary of the Bible. Grand Rapids, MI: David Noel Freeman, Editor–in-Chief

Deuteronomy 28: 1-14 (KJV)

Chagorah(Hebrew): something with which to be gird about, as a belt or girdle. New Strong's Exhaustive Concordance of the Bible, (1995, 1996) Nashville, TN. Thomas Nelson Publishers.

Epithumia (Greek)which means desire, crave, and a longing for what is forbidden; concupiscence-sexual desire. . New Strong's Exhaustive Concordance of the Bible, (1995, 1996) Nashville, TN. Thomas Nelson Publishers.

New American Stand Bible

Baptist Hymnal (1977) "He Will Carry You Through", Nashville, TN: National Baptist Publishing Board

Astheneia (Greek) want of strength; weakness; infirmity: meaning a moral, mental, or physical weakness or flaw. New Strong's Exhaustive Concordance of the Bible, (1995, 1996) Nashville, TN. Thomas Nelson Publishers.

After receiving Christ, we are in it, and into it. You cannot get rid of it once it is in you—this divine power. (Smith Wigglesworth paraphrased) Liardon, R. (1996) Smith Wigglesworth:The Complete Collection of His Life Teachings: Tulsa, OK. Albury Publishing.

Baptist Hymnal, (1977) We've Come This Far By Faith. Nashville, TN: National Baptist Publishing Board

Message Bible

Dake, F. J., (1993) Dake's Annotated Study Bible: Lawrenceville, GA.

Dictionary.com

A.J. Russell, (1989)God Calling, A. J. Russell. Uhrichsville, OH: Barbour Publishing, Inc.

King James Version of the Bible

New American Standard Bible

New International Version of the Bible

New King James Version of the Bible

Soleyn, S. (2012) My Father My Father: Albuquerque, NM: Soleyn Publishing LLC. New Strong's Exhaustive Concordance of the Bible, (1995, 1996) Nashville, TN. Thomas Nelson Publishers.

Liardon, R. (1996) Smith Wigglesworth:The Complete Collection of His Life Teachings: Tulsa, OK. Albury Publishing.

Thorndike Barnhart Advanced Dictionary (1994) Glenview, IL: Scott Foresman & Company

Answer Key

Introduction
Page xi

1. Guilt
2. Shame
3. Blame

God clothed them with coats of skin through the shedding of blood of an innocent lamb. This redemptive solution would have generational implications for all of mankind. Add these statements.

1. Forgive
2. Grace
3. Mercy

Page xii

1. Hiding behind work
2. Hiding in hobbies
3. Hiding in man-caves

True

1. Naked - Being completely nude or without clothing
2. Naked - The loss of being clothed with glory
3. Naked - Condemnation
4. Naked - Deprivation

Overcoming the Stronghold of Condemnation

Overcoming defined is:

1. To get the better of in a struggle or conflict; conquer; defeat—to overcome the enemy.
2. To prevail over (opposition, a debility, temptations, etc.); surmount—to overcome one's weaknesses.

3. To overpower or overwhelm in body or mind, as does liquor, a drug, exertion, or emotion—overcome with guilt.
4. To overspread or overrun.
5. To gain the victory: win; conquer—a plan to overcome by any means possible.

Stronghold defined is:

1. A net
2. A snare

Circle one: Adam

Circle one: Jesus

Many sons of God are not reigning in life victoriously because we are overcome with the stronghold of condemnation. (pp. xii-xiii)

Men who suffer with the affliction of condemnation have placed more emphasis on what Adam did in the Garden of Eden than what Jesus did on Calvary. (p. xiii)

The greatest weapon the enemy has against a man after he has made a confession of faith is condemnation.

Chapter 1
The Fall into Condemnation-Page 17

The Origin of Condemnation

God established Adam as the chief steward, the earthblesser. He had authority over everything God created. God empowered Adam to prosper in all things. (p. 15)

1. Glory
2. Holiness
3. Honor
4. Righteousness

The act of disobedience in the Garden changed how Adam saw himself and how God saw him. In God's eyes, the clothing of glory, holiness, honor, and righteousness were gone. (p. 16)

Adam's reaction to his spiritual demotion and his nakedness introduced guilt, fear, and death to what was formally perfection. (p. 16)

Condemnation and deprivation are the greatest barriers to a man walking in the fullness of his purpose and in the fullness of his calling.

Page 18

1. Shameful
2. Embarrassing
3. Reason to be afraid

Adam's realization of what he had done caused:

1. A deep disappointment he had never experienced
2. Doubt of the excellence and perfection of God
3. What he had lost was greater than what he gained
4. Overwhelming conviction that things would never be the same

Four Important Facts about Condemnation (p. 17)

1. We are born into condemnation.
2. Condemnation is once again associated with The Fall.
3. Condemnation occurred when Adam ate, not Eve.
4. Condemnation originated from and is attributed to the devil.

Sin changed their predominately spiritual condition to a predominately physical condition. They were both overwhelmed with a sense of doom and loss. (p. 18)

Losses Associated with Spiritual Demotion: (p. 18)

1. The ability to see spiritual things
2. Their mind, the God way of thinking
3. Lost their paradise

4. Lost their lifespan
5. Lost their intimacy with God

As such, when a man is under condemnation, it affects his wife and family. However, when a man overcomes the stronghold of condemnation, his salvation blesses his wife and influences the atmosphere in his entire household. (p. 18)

1. We are born into condemnation.
2. Condemnation is once again associated with The Fall.
3. Condemnation occurred when Adam ate, not Eve.
4. Condemnation originated from and is attributed to the devil.

Adam Before the Fall-Page 20

b. 1, 2 and 3

Sin entered creation through Adam. Salvation entered creation through Jesus We are all natural born sinners.

Through Christ, we are born again into righteousness. Men who are still in the nature of Adam are naked.

Men who are in the nature of Christ are clothed. (p. 19)

Page 21

Place a check under the name which corresponds to the description that most accurately distinguish Jesus from Adam. (p. 19)

Description	Adam	Jesus
Son of God		√
Made flesh from dirt		√
Made flesh from Spirit		√
Nature of Sin	√	
Nature of Righteousness		√
Condemnation	√	
Redemption		√
Deprivation	√	
Restoration		√
Naked	√	
Clothed		√

Eerdman's Dictionary definition of naked is: Totally nude or inadequately clothed.

Nakedness is used to described a variety of human conditions associated with our sinful nature, however the two words which categories most of these conditions are condemnation and deprivation (p. 20)

Page 22

All of the above

1. Poverty
2. Oppression
3. Judgment
4. Punishment

Being spiritually clothed or covered is an absolute imperative for meaningful interaction with God. (p.21)

The Fall has created two human conditions which initiated and continues to widen the gap between God and man. The two conditions are condemnation and deprivation. Combined, they constitute the naked condition. (p. 21)

The Naked Condition-Page 23

The naked condition of condemnation describes the adverse spiritual and psychological consequences associated with nakedness. Which of the following are associated with the human condition of condemnation? (p. 21)

All the above

Deprivation is the twin brother of condemnation. It describes the adverse spiritual, psychological and physical losses associated with nakedness. Deprivation is removal from ecclesiastical office with all its provisions and benefits. Which of the following are associated with the human condition of deprivation? (p.22)

All the above

The Clothed Condition-Page 24-25

Being born again changes our human condition and restores a man to his dominate spiritual condition. We die to the nature of Adam—the sin nature. We inherit the nature of Christ—the righteous nature. (p. 24)

To make this plain, match the word to the right phrase. (p. 25)

1. The Son of God
2. Became the Sons of man
3. In order that the sons of men
4. May become the sons of God Son

Jesus
Begotten
Joint-heirs

Page 26

To summarize Chapter 1, match the phrases below:

1.	Naked Condition	b.	a. God-consciousness
2.	Clothed Condition	a.	b. Condemnation
3.	Naked Condition	d.	c. Redeemed
4.	Clothed Condition	c.	d. World-consciousness
5.	Naked Condition	f.	e. Restored
6.	Clothed Condition	e.	f. Deprivation

Chapter 2-Page 28
The Naked

The naked is a phrase which applies to all who are spiritually dead. The place of origin of spiritual death for all humankind is the Garden of Eden. From the time of The Fall until now, all are born spiritually dead. The one who instigated spiritual death is Satan. The progenitor (ancestor) of spiritual death is Adam.

They lost a. spiritual awareness
They became more b. self-conscious

The deceitfulness of sin is the sense we will gain more from the disobedient act than what we already have—that the pleasures of sin are greater than the promises of God.

Page 30

1. Loss of God-way of thinking to man-way of thinking
2. Man's view of nakedness over God's view of nakedness
3. Loss of God-consciousness

The Naked Mentality-Page 30

The naked mentality of this sort becomes a conscious choice made by a believer and is commonly referred to as self-condemnation and self- deprivation. It is a decision to not accept what Christ has done, even after coming into the knowledge of the truth. (p. 32)

All the above

The naked mentality exists when sons of God feel the strength of our salvation only between transgressions. In other words, we only feel saved until the next time we mess up, then we feel condemned all over again. (p.33)

Salvation is continuous, ongoing, and everlasting.

We are not forgiven for the time being. We are forgiven forevermore. We are not saved to the almost. We are saved to the utmost.

Page 31

1. True
2. True
3. True
4. True
5. True

Page 32

1. Careers and jobs
2. Hobbies
3. Business success
4. Political success

1. Expects something bad to happen C
2. Expects something good to happen S
3. Is rooted in fear and doubt C
4. Is rooted in faith and confidence S
5. Is hell on earth C
6. Is heaven on earth S

Page 33

Name five indicators of the naked mentality. (p. 37)

1. Guilt
2. Cover up
3. Blame
4. Discouragement
5. Lack of accountability

1. World-consciousness
2. Self-consciousness
3. God-consciousness

Chapter 3-Page 36
The Need for Covering

1. God made Adam and Eve coats of skin
2. The lamb had to die
3. The lamb's blood was shed
4. The lamb was sacrificed by God

1. God initiated animal sacrifices
2. God chose a perfect lamb

3. The lamb was innocent
4. God set the precedent for animal sacrifices

Page 37

Putting on Christ is a renewing of the mind, a constant awareness of our clothed condition. Circle the human condition that is not aligned within the proper column.

Discovering the Human Condition of Nakedness

1.	I was afraid b	a. guilt discovered
2.	I was naked c	b. fear discovered
3.	I hid myself a	c. shame discovered

The Human Condition Before and After Sin

Before Sin	**After Sin**
Afraid of God	Courageous in God
Confident	Ashamed
Guilty before God	Innocent in God
Clothed	Naked

The Origin of Doubt-Page 38

One of the consequences of our depraved condition is we still have the propensity to doubt the truth of God, especially when the truth of God conflict with the desires of our carnal nature. (p. 46)

The question raised by the serpent, "hath God said, ye shall not eat of every tree of the garden?" was asked with the specific intent of questioning the credibility and authenticity of the Word of God. The serpent's reply to Eve's affirmative response based on the truth was, "you shall not surely die".

1. Sarah
2. Moses
3. Gideon
4. Saul
5. Thomas

Page 39

1. True
2. True
3. True
4. True
5. False

The Origin of Fear-Page 40

As a result of Adam's experience, men today have many phobias— persistent irrational fears of a specific object, activity, or situations which leads to a compelling desire to avoid them—most of which have little or no chance of actually happening.

Fear is a distressing emotion aroused by impending danger, evil, or pain whether the threat is real or imagined.

Fear is the feeling or condition of being afraid.

The fears born out of the sinful nature have caused many men to completely alter their lifestyle, resulting in behaviors which limit the capacity of God to manifest his fullness in their lives. (p. 48)

[Complete the following sentences by filling in the blanks.]

Fear of commitment causes a man to go from one relationship to another, never get married, and go from one job to another.
Fear of failure causes a man to not take risks which build his independence and wealth resulting in a mediocre life.
Self-disclosure causes a man to refrain from sharing personal challenges with family and friends.

The Origin of Blame-Page 41

The loss of Adam's spiritual nature created the infamous couple of fear and shame which conceived and gave birth to yet another consequence of our depraved condition—blame.

1. True
2. True
3. True

Chapter 4-Page 45
The Significance of Clothes (p.55)

The primary purpose of clothing from the beginning until now is to: cover nakedness and to be presentable before God and people.

1. True
2. True
3. False

When a man is inappropriately dressed he is insecure, unsure, and lacks confidence. (p. 56)

If a man shows up at an event that has a specific dress code and is the only man in the wrong attire, he is and embarrassed and ashamed.

These are the same emotional responses Adam experienced in the Garden of Eden and are consequences of condemnation or nakedness.

Jesus Clothes-Page 46

All the above occasions

All the above

1. Distinguish us from other people.
2. Attire provide commensurate with status.
3. Appropriate for every day on duty.
4. The full amour of God is protective clothing.

1. I am the righteousness of God through Christ.
2. I am being conformed to the image of Christ.
3. I am a follower pursuing my purpose.
4. I am forgetting those things which are behind.

5. I am pressing toward the high calling of God.

Chapter 5-Page 50
The Distinction Between the Clothed and the Naked

The biblical distinctions make it clear—a man is either clothed through what Jesus did on Calvary or naked through what Adam did in the Garden of Eden. We cannot be double-minded with regard
to our status of adornment before the Lord, thinking one minute we are clothed and the next minute we are naked. That man will not receive anything from the Lord. (p. 64)

The life of the clothed man is blessed. The life of the naked man is cursed. (p. 65)

Distinctions Between The Clothed and The Naked

The Clothed Man	**The Naked Man**
Righteous	Sinner
Upright	Wicked
Perfect	Ungodly
Just	Worker of Iniquity
Good Man	Scorner
Diligent	Slothful
Blessed	Cursed
	Evildoer

The biblical distinctions make it clear—a man is either blessed through what Jesus did on Calvary or cursed through what Adam did in the Garden of Eden. We cannot be double-minded with regard to our status of adornment before the Lord—thinking one minute we are clothed and the next minute we are naked. That man will not receive anything from the Lord. (p. 64)

The life of the clothed man is blessed. The life of the naked man is cursed. (p. 65)

Page 51

From the Book of Deuteronomy 28, list five blessings of the clothed man.

1. Blessed in the city.
2. Blessed in the country.
3. Blessed children.
4. Blessed household.
5. Blessed in your profession.

From the Book of Deuteronomy 28, list five curses of the naked man.

1. Cursed in the city.
2. Cursed in the country.
3. Cursed on children.
4. Cursed household.
5. Cursed in his profession.

Chapter 6-Page 54
Conviction and Condemnation

Conviction comes through God-consciousness.
Condemnation comes through sin-consciousness.
Conviction is the awareness of God at the time of temptation to choose God's way.
Condemnation is a predominant awareness of the sinful nature and a compelling sense of being defeated by it.
Conviction is the Holy Spirit reminding us of the commandments, precepts, statutes, and laws of God which illuminate the way out of temptation.
Condemnation is a reminder of what Adam did in the Garden of Eden.
Conviction is a reminder of what Jesus did on Calvary.

b. He brings promotions and advancements as he has promised according to our faithfulness to him.

Page 55

No

Conviction is at work before, during and after a transgression

Conviction is a: blessing.

Both statements summarize the truth about conviction.

All the above

Page 56

Condemnation is a curse.

Both statements summarize the truth about condemnation.

Both choices are faced following a transgression

Condemnation is our enemy, our adversary, and a constant agitator, deceiver, and tempter, trying to convince us that we are still naked.

Conviction is our companion and advocate; a very present help; a constant counselor of salvation's benefits, righteousness and reminder that we are clothed with Christ.

Page 57

1. Peter: Convicted
2. Judas: Condemned

The lesson here is, a naked man cannot recognize the voice of Jesus. A clothed man has to make it known to him. Peter was spiritually clothed by had a naked mindset due to condemnation.

As clothed men, we must never allow the weight of our conviction to lead to condemnation.

Chapter 7-Page 60
The State of Depravity

1. All the above

2. "The Lord God formed man of the dust from the ground, and breathed into his nostrils the breath of life, and man became a living being." Genesis 2:7

"The Lord God planted a garden and there he placed the man whom he formed." Genesis 2:8

3. a. The Lord God formed man.
   b. The Lord God planted a garden.
   c. The Lord provided every tree in the garden.
   d. The Lord took the man and put him in the garden.

Page 61

4. Death occurred when Adam ate—not when Eve ate.

5. Both A and B are correct.

6. All but A are correct

7. All the above

Page 62

8. In the text we read that lust is a passionate, overwhelming desire or craving for things such as power, prestige, money, and other possessions. Fill in the blanks in the sentence below. (p. 78)

The most common use of the word "lust" is in the context of intense sexual desire or appetite; or uncontrolled, illicit sensual desire.

Lust Originates in the Heart

9. All of the above

10. Self-pleasure
    Self-aggrandizement
    Self-exaltation

Page 63

11. Sensuality drives the personality of a naked man

Spirituality drives the personality of a clothed man

Page 64

13. Sex outside of God's plan and purpose always leaves a man empty.

14. Since procreation is a spiritual act between carnal beings, God intended it to occur only in the institution of holy matrimony—marriage.

    a. As such, since God made sex for procreation, he only intended it to be between a man and a woman.

15. All the above

Page 65

16. When a man's eyes lack spiritual discipline it will lead him to lust for women, lust for other men, covetousness, idolatry and all kinds of desires and evils. Fill in the blanks. (p. 87)

    a. The scriptures encourage us to guard our heart, for out of it flows the issues of life.

    b. Men should be even more diligent to guard their eyes, for they are the entry point to a man's soul which stores up the things that come out of our heart.

17. a. Convicted by even the thought of the visual transgression and does not want it to go any further.

Clothed Man

    b. Does not consider the consequences. In some cases, he actually does, but is willing to take the risks.

Naked Man

18. True

19. All of the above

Page 66

20. Jeremiah 29:11:"I know the plans I have for you says the Lord; plans to prosper you, not to harm you; to give you a future and a hope."

21. True

22. God only has a plan for our prestige

Page 67

24. All the above.

25. Naked man

Page 68

26. The blessing of the Lord makes one rich, and he adds no sorrow with it.

27. A naked man

28. Both A and B are True

Page 69

29. The prodigal son

30. The basic, all-purpose garment of a Clothed Man is love.

Chapter 8-Page 72
Lead Us Not into Temptation

Every man is tempted with lust of the flesh, lust of the eyes and with pride. Each of us have our vulnerabilities and our weaknesses. We all have repressed sensations etched in our flesh from the days before we committed our lives to Christ. Many of us are challenged with how long to look at a beautiful woman without allowing lust to be conceived, or how long to look in awe at certain material possessions of others without being covetous. Additionally, there are those among our ranks who wrestle with aspirations of success and achievement whose motive is not for the glory of God but to glorify self. In spite of these truths, we should not be discouraged. Jesus was tempted at all points as we are, yet without sin (Hebrews 4:15). Because Jesus was victorious over temptation, we too have the victory.

1. Every man is tempted with lust of the flesh, lust of the eyes, and with pride. There are those among our ranks who wrestle with aspirations of success and achievement whose motives is not for the glory of God but to glorify self.

    a. True
    b. False

Page 73

2. We fall when we allow ourselves to be drawn away, caught up in the moment, and linger in the thought processes that lead to the conception of lust. (p. 98)

    a. If we give place, linger, dwell, permit the opportunity for prolonged exposure to our vulnerabilities and weaknesses, we are at the risk of being drawn away into our own lust.

3. All the above

4. All the above

5. Both A & B

Page 74

6. Circle the correct answer.

Both A and B

7. a. A naked man has resigned to the sinful nature and is content being naked.

    b. A clothed man diligently fights, and is never satisfied with transgression (wrongdoing).

Page 75

1. a. Those who would live ungodly lives thereafter.

2. a. The Lord knows how to rescue the godly out of temptation, and to reserve the unjust unto the Day of Judgment.

3. James 1:14-15 says:

"But every man is tempted, when his drawn away of his own lust, and enticed. Then when hath conceived, it bringeth forth sin: and sin, when it is finished, bringeth forth death."

4. James 1:12 says:

Page 76

"Blessed is the man that endures temptation: for when he is tried, he shall receive the crown of life, which the Lord hath promised to them that love him."

13. Through the Holy Spirit

The Escape Route

No

True

14.

a. True

b. False

Chapter 9-Page 80
The Wrestling Match

1. Principalities, powers, rulers of the darkness of this world, spiritual wickedness and high places.

2. The messenger of Satan.

3. To buffet and bewray.

4. Humility

Page 81

5. Conviction. “Lest I be exalted above measure through the abundance of revelations.

6. My grace is sufficient for thee: for my strength is made perfect in weakness.

The Issue of Infirmities

7. Yes

8. Seventeen

Page 82

10.

a. Satan is not intimidated by your anointing if he has control of your character.

b. Samson’s temptation and depravity kept taking him back to the same kind of woman.

c. When a clothed man persists in dabbling in his infirmities and does not put up a good fight of faith with temptation, God releases him to his own demise.

Chapter 10-Page 84
Work Out Your Soul Salvation

1. All the above

2. His lifestyle should be morel. That of a passionate athlete, but with spiritual exercises and spiritual goals.

3. a. Be a willing participant.

a. Have a life consecrated to God.

Page 85

All the above.

4. All are motivating factors for a clothed man's work out.

We Have a Coach

5.	Facilities	Place of Worship
	Work out Session	Small Groups
	Dietary Plan	Fasting Prayer
	Personal Trainers	Pastors, Teachers, Mentors

The Diligence of the Clothed Man

Page 86

6. a. Constant and earnest in their efforts to accomplish what has been undertaken
   b. Persistent and attentive in the disciplines necessary to achieve their destiny
   c. Hardworking and industrious
   d. Careful and steady in all their decisions, persevering through difficult assignments

7.	Time Worshipping	Subject to Accountability
	Feeding on Word	Embrace Lessons Learned
	Fasting	Reconciliation

Chapter 11-Page 88
The Disciplined Life of a Clothed Man

Walking in the Spirit

1. a. Sustains us spiritually
   b. Does the work in us
   c. Makes us righteous

2. The Spirit of God dwells in a clothed man.

3. All are descriptions of "walking in the Spirit".

4. All are descriptions of "walking in the flesh".

Page 89

5. Walking in the Flesh

6. Walking in the Spirit

7. All the above

Page 89-90

8. Step 1: Daily quiet time
Step 2: Prayer and fasting
Step 3: Daily feeding on the Word of God
Step 4: Wholesome relationships with family and friends
Step 5: Accountability to others

9. Daily quiet time is all about spending time with God.

10. A clothed man should pray one time a day-all day long.

11. A combination of prayer and fasting invokes a greater level of spiritual awareness, power and sensitivity to the guidance of the Holy Spirit. (p. 136)

12. As clothed men we must establish a way of life where we are consistent in feeding our spirit-man of God's word. (p. 137)

13. False

14. His Family

Chapter 12-Page 94
A Spirit-Filled Virtuous Life

1. What is the compelling evidence of a lifestyle of a clothed man? Explain. (p. 143)
It is a life manifesting God's glory and virtue in all roles, relationships and responsibilities of manhood.

Called to Glory

1. All are definitions of glory
2. Love, joy, peace, patience, kindness, goodness, faithfulness, gentleness, and self-control.

Page 95

15. a. Glory,
    b. Virtue

5. Faith and virtue sustains our victory over condemnation and conviction.

Chapter 13-Page 98
We Have Overcome the Stronghold of Condemnation

1. We continue to treat sin as an incurable disease.

2. His victory on Calvary was our victory. He did what we could not do for ourselves. In his conquering power we walk victorious and unharmed today.

3. True

4. Christ gives us victory over condemnation.

Page 99

5. When a clothed man overcomes it brings salvation to his entire household.

6. Clothed men serving from the heart are predominately filled.
(p. 156)

7. Naked, self-serving men are predominately deprived.

8. Both a & d

9. The naked, love, darkness, the works of the flesh, and the pleasures of sin more than light.

The clothed, love, the works of the spirit and the pleasures of righteous and therefore walk in the light.

www.ingramcontent.com/pod-product-compliance
Lightning Source LLC
Chambersburg PA
CBHW080533090426
42733CB00015B/2575
* 9 7 8 1 9 4 1 2 4 7 5 4 9 *